Entrepreneur® MAGAZINE'S

startup

Start Your Own

CRAFTS BUSINESS

Your Step-by-Step Guide to Success

Jacquelyn Lynn

EP
Entrepreneur
Press

Editorial Director: Jere L. Calmes
Managing Editor: Marla Markman
Cover Design: Beth Hansen-Winter
Production: Eliot House Productions
Composition: Ed Stevens

This publication is designed to provide accurate and authoritative information in regard to the subject matter covered. It is sold with the understanding that the publisher is not engaged in rendering legal, accounting or other professional services. If legal advice or other expert assistance is required, the services of a competent professional person should be sought.

Library of Congress Cataloging-in-Publication Data

Lynn, Jacquelyn.
    Entrepreneur magazine's start up: start your own crafts business/by Jacquelin Lynn.—[3rd ed.].
       p. cm. —(Entrepreneur magazine's start-up series ; guide #1304)
"This book is the third edition of How to start a crafts business and is a completely revised and expanded version"—P.
    Includes index.
    ISBN 1-891984-92-6
       1. Handicraft industries—Management. 2. New business enterprises—Management. 3. Home-based businesses—Management. I. Title: Start your own crafts business. II. Title: Crafts business. III. Entrepreneur Media, Inc. IV. Entrepreneur (Santa Monica, Calif.) V. Title. VI. Entrepreneur business start-up guide ; no. 1304.

HD9999.H362L95 2003
680'.68'1--dc22   2003063079

Printed in Canada

09 08 07 06 05 04   10 9 8 7 6 5 4 3 2 1

Contents

▲

Preface

Regardless of the particular type of crafts business you want to start, this book will tell you how to do it. We'll start with an overview of the industry, look at some specific crafts businesses, and then go through the step-by-step process of setting up and running your new venture.

You'll learn about basic requirements and start-up costs, daily operations, and what to do when things don't go according to plan. You'll gain a solid understanding of the sales and marketing process, as well as how to track and manage the financial side of your business. Throughout the book, you'll hear

▲

from crafters who have built successful operations and are eager to share what they learned in the process.

Whether you plan to start a part-time business by yourself or you want to jump into crafting full time and hire employees, we recommend that you read every chapter in this book, because most of the information applies to all sizes and types of crafts businesses, and the information is interrelated.

The market for crafts is tremendous, but it's also extremely competitive, which means you need a plan to set yourself apart. Something else you need to keep in mind is that the opportunity to express yourself creatively is virtually limitless, but sometimes you have to just do what the customer asks, even if it's not your preference, to make a sale. That's part of being in business instead of just having a hobby.

Like anything else, there's no magic formula, no quick path to success. Your crafts business will definitely not be a get-rich-quick operation. But it can be a substantial revenue-generator for you.

Because we believe business should be fun as well as profitable, we designed this book to be logical, informative, and entertaining. We want you to enjoy yourself as you read. Just one word of warning: Take the time to sit back and relax now, because once your crafts business is up and running, you're going to be a very busy person!

1

Making It
Yourself

Assembly lines around the world are churning out mass-produced items that are purchased almost as fast as they can be made. But consumer acceptance of low-cost, look-alike goods hasn't eliminated the demand for handcrafted items—although those items are likely to have a much different function today than in the past.

Many handcrafted items are now valued as works of art, but historically their value was primarily utilitarian. For example, baskets and pottery were essential for transporting food, water, and other items. And weaving produced fabrics that could be made into clothing and blankets.

Because of the industrial revolution, the need for functional handcrafted items is not as extensive as it once was. But Americans who want quality artistic and decorative items turn to modern-day craftspeople who produce a variety of items such as jewelry, ceramics, wood carvings, furniture, crocheted and knitted goods, decorated clothing, toys, and much more.

What Is a Craft?

In this book, *craft* refers to any handmade item that can be given as a gift or sold— and if you've attended a crafts fair, you may have been surprised by what craftspeople sell and what people are willing to buy. The unpredictability of the crafts market is one of the intriguing and challenging aspects of the business.

In *Craft Today: Poetry of the Physical*, Paul J. Smith writes, "In its broadest sense craft refers to the creation of original objects through an artist's disciplined manipulation of material. Historically craft was identified with producing objects that were necessary to life. Modern industrialized society eliminates the need to make by hand essentials for living. The term *craft* now must be defined in the context of a society that focuses on greater efficiency by technological achievement."

The question of whether crafts are art or a separate medium may never be definitively answered. In *The Crafts of the Modern World*, Rose Slivka writes, "Throughout their long history, crafts have produced useful objects which are later considered fine art. Time has a way of overwhelming the functional value of an object that outlives the men who made and used it, with the power of its own objective presence—that life-invest quality of being that transcends and energizes. When this happens, such objects are forever honored for their own sakes—they are art."

Of course, for someone wanting to start a crafts business, the question of whether the products are art may not be particularly important. A more critical question is whether you can make money.

The nature of the crafts industry makes it difficult to define and quantify, but industry

Stat Fact

According to the Hobby Industry Association, more than four out of five U.S. households have at least one family member engaged in crafts/hobbies; 77 percent use their crafts as gifts, 71 percent for personal use, 63 percent specifically for home decorating, 47 percent for holiday decorations. Fifteen percent sell their crafts.

experts estimate that sales revenues exceed $10 billion annually, and hundreds of thousands of working artisans earn their entire income from the crafts they produce.

Most professional craftspeople start making their handcrafted goods as a hobby, and begin selling items to friends and family. From there, they typically expand to selling in crafts shows and fairs several times a year. Sometimes they're content to keep this as something they do on the side; others are eager to move from part-time to full-time status. Still other artisans tackle their work as a full-time career from the beginning, often renting studio or retail space, or both.

Start-up costs for a crafts business range from literally a few dollars to several thousand dollars, depending on what you are making, what type of equipment and raw materials you need, and whether you already own equipment when you start. Crafters earn as little as a few dollars an hour (for part-time crafters who are not particularly interested in profits) to as much as $20 or $30 an hour and sometimes more if they learn how to market and manage their businesses efficiently.

In the Beginning

Let's take a look at how some established craftspeople got started: Jay Norman of DeLand, Florida, who makes containers for his business, Organize with Wood, was a dance teacher who had worked with wood as a hobby all his life. He says his wife, Dianne, turned him into a professional craftsperson. "His items were so clever and unusual, I thought he could sell them," she recalls. So Jay and Dianne quit their jobs in New York in 1997, moved to Florida, and now sell virtually year-round at crafts shows around the country.

Judy Infinger of Altamonte Springs, Florida, makes wood and fabric decorative items, primarily with a Christmas theme, for her part-time business, Woods and Threads, which she started back in 1988. "I just do fall shows, so I concentrate on Christmas items—ornaments, pins, that sort of thing—which are my favorite, anyway," she says. She builds her inventory throughout the year, then sells at shows during the autumn crafts show season.

Deborah Farish, owner of Dolls by Deb of Manchester, Missouri, makes soft-sculptured dolls as a part-time business and works full time as an administrative assistant in an accounting firm. She's been sewing since she was 12. "I would go to crafts shows, look at

Stat Fact

How much do consumers spend on crafts as gifts? According to the National Craft Association, when the item is for themselves, relatives, or close friends, they spend $20 to $30; when it's for other adults or children on their gift list, they spend $10 to $20; when it's a token gift for co-workers, teachers, professional or service providers, they spend $5 to $10.

dolls, and think, 'I can do that'—which is what everybody says when they go to a crafts show," she says. Finally, in 1993, she bought some fabric, made a doll she took into her office as a sample, and began getting orders. With the encouragement of friends and customers, she built an inventory and began exhibiting at crafts shows.

Gladys Johnson of Bunn, North Carolina, was looking for a hobby when a friend of hers invited her to a doll-making class. "After doing my first doll, I was hooked," she says. Still, in the beginning, she had no intention of turning her hobby into the business she named Dolls by Gladys. But in 1995 "it got to the point where I had to get rid of some of the dolls so I could make more," she explains. She makes porcelain dolls, most with cloth bodies (although she has made some with porcelain bodies).

Lynn Korff, owner of Korff's Ceramic Originals in Cabot, Pennsylvania, had been making ceramics for about six years when she opened her own studio and shop where

---

A Day in the Life

Atypical day for a part-time craftsperson will, of course, differ significantly from that of a full-time crafter. Many part-time crafters have full-time jobs they must work around. Typically, crafters who exhibit in shows spend their weekdays making their products and their weekends at shows.

Deb Farish of Dolls by Deb in Manchester, Missouri, says finding the time to do it all is her biggest challenge. "Beyond sitting at a craft show for eight hours on a Saturday and Sunday, there's trying to juggle a full-time job, raising children and their pets, the laundry, watering the plants, and then finding a few hours to spend at the sewing machine or hot glue center, or whatever you need to do. It's very difficult."

There's much more to having a crafts business than simply making the items. You need to allow time to shop for and purchase your raw materials. You'll also need to spend time doing research to determine which crafts shows are best for you, and putting together the applications to exhibit in those shows. You need to develop and implement an effective marketing plan. And, of course, there's administration: record-keeping, maintaining the required licenses and permits, payroll (if you have employees), taxes, and so on. These are not tasks that crafts-people are typically good at or enjoy. But they must be done.

If it sounds like a crafts business is hard work, it is. What's more, it's not an industry with wide profit margins. So why do it? Deb says, "It's fun, it's relaxing. I'm a happy person, but I'm even happier because I can create something, make somebody smile, touch somebody by what I have made. And if somebody likes it enough to buy it and give it to someone else, or put it in their own home—that's such a kick."

she made ceramics, held classes and sold supplies. Eleven years later, she decided to downsize: She closed the shop, moved her business home and set up a Web site in 1999 to sell her crafts. Her primary product is piggy banks, but she also makes and custom paints other ceramic items, such as dinnerware, flower pots, candle holders, serving dishes, and specialty plates.

A love of candles prompted Melony Bell of Fort Meade, Florida, to start making them as a hobby. She wasn't satisfied with the quality of candles available in stores. Her husband is a beekeeper, so she started using his beeswax to make her own candles. After she gave a few as gifts, people started asking if they could buy her candles. So, in 1998 with a full-time job as an auditor with the Florida Division of Motor Vehicles and serving as city commissioner/mayor for her town, she started her own candle-making company.

> ### Bright Idea
> Before you leap from hobby to business, take an informal poll of your friends. Ask them how much they would expect to pay (not if they would buy) for your crafts. That will give a very unscientific idea of your potential price point and whether or not you'll be able to recover your material costs and still make a profit.

Anita Fetter of Waynesfield, Ohio, has been making and selling wood and fabric crafts since 1980. She started working with her husband, who made wood items that she painted or stained; she also did cross-stitch, knitted, and made stuffed animals. But as their hobby turned into a business, her husband backed out of it. "He stopped when it got to be a job," she says. "Now I do most of it and just make things for the fall and winter."

What these crafters and many others have found is that while selling their handcrafted goods is often fairly easy, the challenge is making a profit. You need to decide what to make, determine if there is a sufficient market for that item, then figure out if you have the wherewithal to reach that market. Just because your family members appreciate your handmade gifts and your co-workers are willing to buy modestly priced items from you doesn't necessarily mean you can sell enough of them at a price that will justify your investment of materials and time. On the other hand, friends and family may be just the proverbial tip of the iceberg, and you may have a product that will become the foundation for a thriving company.

Beyond that is the issue of running a business. Just because you love doing a particular craft doesn't mean you'll love doing all the things that go with running a crafts business. Of course, you don't have to *love* them, but you do have to *do* them.

2

Taking the
First Steps

The first step is, of course, deciding what crafts you're going to make. It's a choice that is entirely up to you. Chances are, you already have an idea of the type of crafts you want to do, but let's take a look at the more popular ones:

▲

- *Ceramics.* Ceramists most commonly make vases and mugs, but you can also make dishes, plaques, ornaments, and other items.
- *Floral crafts.* These comprise any items made from artificial or dried flowers, including table arrangements, wall decorations, and bouquets.
- *Candle-making.* Candles are popular and consumable, which means your customers use them and come back to you for more.
- *Jewelry.* You can make all types of jewelry—rings, necklaces, bracelets, earrings, and items for various body parts—in any price range using a variety of materials.
- *Sewing.* Sewn crafts include a broad range of items, such as clothing, stuffed animals, home furnishings, and linens.
- *Needlecraft.* Needlecraft includes cross-stitch and needlepoint. You can make wall hangings, table runners, holiday decorations, napkins, and tablecloths.
- *Crocheting and knitting.* You can crochet and knit various items, such as blankets, clothing, and decorative accessories.
- *Woodworking.* You can make a wide range of items from wood, including toys, furniture, and various decorative items.
- *Wood carving.* Wood-carvers fashion wood to represent animals, people, or artistic designs.
- *Glass.* Artisans who work with glass typically make either stained glass or glass sculptures and vases.

One of the attractions of operating your own crafts business is that you can make what you want and you are not limited to one type of item. In fact, experienced craftspeople recommend that you either offer variations of the item or make several different types of crafts. For example, if you make wreaths, don't make all of them out of grapevine; make some out of straw. If you make jewelry, don't limit yourself to necklaces; also offer bracelets, rings, and earrings.

If your product lends itself, offer a variety of sizes, shapes, and colors. For example, if you make ceramic vases, don't make them all alike—no matter how much you like a particular design, give your customers a choice.

What Does It Take?

What does it take to be a successful crafter? First and foremost, love what you do and be good at it, crafters say. Deb Farish, a doll maker in Manchester, Missouri, says years of sewing experience and knowing how to follow pattern directions have helped her. "I've made wedding dresses, curtains, baby clothes, and my own clothes. The experience working with fabrics and patterns—so that I cannot only follow the directions but develop shortcuts that save time and money—has come in handy," she says.

But it's about more than the practical. "The best experience is sewing, but the bigger thing is the love of dolls. I had a giant collection of dolls when I was a child. Our basement flooded, and I lost them all. I guess I never recovered, but now I have a giant collection of dolls again. I make some, and I buy other people's."

Judy Infinger's father did woodworking, so the crafter in Altamonte Springs, Florida, grew up around it. "But there was nothing specific he showed me, I just decided to start being creative," she says. While she has made some items using patterns, she says, "My best sellers are the things that I came up with the idea for myself."

Anita Fetter, who makes wood and fabric crafts in Waynesfield, Ohio, had worked in a fabric store for ten years, and learned a lot about sewing and crafts there. "I have always liked to work with my hands," she says.

Because most of your time will be spent doing the craft of your choice, make it something you love.

It also helps to have some sense of how to run a business. You might prefer to walk across hot coals than create financial statements or a marketing plan, but if you don't know how to do those things, it won't matter how good your crafts are. And the first step in running a business is planning it.

Bright Idea

Always have something new in your craft show booth so people who have visited before don't pass you by thinking they've seen all you have to offer. For example, one year doll maker Deb Farish made cheerleading dolls based on the football teams in the Superbowl. "Stay with your core, but add something new to bring people back in," she says.

Put It in Writing

Some entrepreneurs will do just about anything to avoid sitting down and writing a business plan. Other would-be business owners get so caught up in planning every detail that they never get their businesses off the ground. You need to find a happy medium between these two extremes.

Begin your venture with a written business plan. Writing down your plan forces you to think it through and gives you a chance to examine it for consistency and thoroughness. Whether you've got years of crafting experience

Smart Tip

Tip...

Don't just write your business plan and put it away; use it to guide your daily operation. Update the plan every year: Choose a date when you sit down with your plan, compare how closely your actual operation and results mirrored your forecasts, and decide if your plans for the coming year need adjusting.

▲

behind you or you're a novice in the industry, you need a plan for your business. This chapter will focus on issues particular to planning crafts businesses, but they are by no means all you need to consider when writing your plan. See Chapter 3 in *Start-Up Basics* for complete guidelines on how to put together a general business plan.

Business Plans 101

Though the specific content of your business plan will be unique, there is a basic format that you should follow to assure you address all the necessary issues. Include these elements:

❍ *Front matter.* This includes your cover page, a table of contents, and a statement of purpose.

❍ *Business description.* Describe the specific crafts business you intend to start, and list the reasons you can make it successful. This section should also include your business philosophy, goals, industry analysis, operations, inventory, and start-up timetable.

❍ *Marketing plan.* Include an overview of the market, describe your potential customers, discuss the advantages and drawbacks of your location, analyze the competition, and show how you plan to promote your specific business.

❍ *Company organization.* Describe your management structure, your staffing needs and how you expect to meet them, the consultants and advisors who will be assisting you, your legal structure, and the licenses, permits, and other regulatory issues that will affect your operations.

❍ *Financial data.* This is where you show the source(s) of your start-up capital and how you're going to use the money. Include information on real estate, fixtures, equipment, and insurance. You'll also include your financial statements: balance sheet, profit-and-loss statement, break-even analysis, personal financial statements, and personal federal income tax returns.

❍ *Financial projections.* Take your financial data and project it out to show what your business will do. Include projected income statements for three years, and cash flow statements for three years, along with worst-case income and cash flow statements to show what you'll do if your plan doesn't work.

❍ *Summary.* Bring your plan together in this section.

❍ *Appendices.* Use this for supporting documents, such as your facility design and layout, marketing studies, sample advertising, copies of leases, and licensing information.

If you're excited about your business, creating a business plan should be an exciting process. It will help you define and evaluate the overall feasibility of your concept, clarify your goals, and determine what you'll need for start-up and long-term operations.

This is a living, breathing document that will provide you with a road map for your company. You'll use it as a guide, referring to it regularly as you work through the start-up process and during the operation of your business. And if you're going to be seeking outside financing, either in the form of loans or investors, your business plan will be the tool that convinces funding sources of your venture's worth.

> ### Smart Tip
> Tip...
>
> When you think your plan is complete, look at it with a fresh eye. Is it realistic? Does it take into account all the possible variables that could affect your operation? After you're satisfied, ask two or three professional associates you trust to evaluate your plan. Use their input to correct any problems before you invest time and money.

Take your time developing your plan; whether you want to start a part-time solo crafts business that never gets any larger or build a sizeable operation, you're making a serious commitment, and you shouldn't rush into it.

Turning Pro

Most of the crafters we interviewed had made at least some of their crafts just for fun before starting their businesses, and they all knew of others who started out as hobbyists. One of the biggest pitfalls of taking this route to business ownership is failing to make the complete transition from amateur to professional.

No matter how much pleasure you derive from doing your craft, this is a product your customers are paying money for, and you must respect the fact that this is a business transaction. It may be tempting to undercut prices both to get new business and because you enjoy making your products so much you'd do it whether you got paid or not, but that's a bad business strategy. It will hurt your business individually and the industry collectively, because you make it more difficult for others to charge fair prices—even long after you've given up because you didn't make any money.

If you've been making your craft as a hobby and have decided to turn that hobby into a

> ### Smart Tip
> Tip...
>
> Once you're made the decision to turn your hobby into a business, give your business the respect it deserves and insist that your family and friends do the same. Don't minimize what you do because it used to be "just a hobby." It's your business now, and should be treated as such.

profitable business, you need to take yourself seriously and run your company like the professional operation you want it to be.

One of the most important issues you'll have to deal with is record-keeping. "When you want to buy something for your hobby, you just do it—it doesn't matter if you pay with cash or credit card, or if you keep the receipt," says Vicki Helmick, CPA. "But in business, those details are critical."

Whether you're turning your hobby into a business, or simply starting a business because this is what you want to do, Helmick offers these suggestions:

- *Open a separate checking account for the business.* Your bank account balance is a quick and easy way to see how well you're doing, but you won't have a clear picture unless you're using an account that is strictly for business income and expenses.

- *Get a credit card for the business.* You may not be able to get the card in the business name, but at least have one card that is used exclusively for business expenses. This helps you keep your records in order and—if the card is in the business name—helps you establish business credit.

- *Invest in a retirement plan.* Beyond the long-term benefits, a retirement plan offers some short-term advantages. You'll not only reduce your current taxes, but if you are a homebased sole proprietor, the fact that you show a retirement plan on your income tax return indicates to the IRS that you are serious about your business, not just trying to take some questionable deductions.

- *Document your equipment.* If you purchased craft equipment as part of your hobby and can prove the cost involved, you may be able to deduct those expenses on your tax return after you've formed your company. Talk to your tax advisor for specifics on how to do this.

- *Figure out how much it costs you to make a product.* Besides the cost of the materials, calculate overhead, your time, freight, special handling, and any other expenses. Be especially careful about tracking your time—too many business owners in all industries fail to give their time the value it deserves.

Identifying the People
Who Will Buy from You

Once you've decided what you're going to
make, you need to figure out who is going to buy it. Your market
is made up of the group of prospective customers who have the
need or desire for your products and the ability to pay for them.
The overall market for handcrafted goods falls into two basic
areas: retail and wholesale. When you retail your products, you

sell direct to the end consumer—that is, the person who buys the product will either keep it or give it as a gift, but will not resell it. When you wholesale your products, you are selling them to a middleman who marks up the price and resells it, typically to the end consumer, but possibly to still another middleman.

Retail Market

The retail or consumer market for handcrafted goods consists predominantly of adult females who are interested in purchasing items with which to decorate their homes or to give as gifts. Handcrafted items can range from inexpensive refrigerator magnets or small ceramic vases, to higher-priced items such as blankets or clothing, to more costly items such as furniture and jewelry. Crafters who exhibit at crafts shows have noted that they have a steady business even when the economy is slow, as long as their items are reasonably priced. When the economy is strong, customers spend their money more freely, buying more expensive goods produced by professional craftspeople.

Wholesale Market

Retail stores are the most common wholesale customer for crafters, and they are a substantial market. You can either sell your goods to them outright at wholesale prices, or sell on consignment. Several types of retail stores may carry handcrafted goods purchased from independent crafters:

- Bridal shops would be most interested in veils, bouquets made of artificial flowers, and related wedding items.
- Clothing stores might be interested in carrying children's clothing, baby accessories, and even women's garments.
- Department stores might carry clothing, blankets, and other home furnishings.
- Drug stores often carry inexpensive gift and decorative items such as refrigerator magnets and small vases.
- Florists might be interested in carrying general craft goods and decorator items such as vases, dried flower arrangements, bird houses, and wreaths.
- Furniture stores might carry handcrafted furniture and accessories.
- Gift shops and souvenir stores typically carry inexpensive items such as small vases, costume jewelry, dolls, and refrigerator magnets.

- Hobby shops and toy stores look for toys and games.
- Stationery stores often stock small and inexpensive gift items.
- Tobacco shops might carry crafts that can be given to men as gifts, such as shaving mugs and engraved items.
- Women's clothing stores might carry jewelry and some handmade clothing.

Bright Idea

Areas that attract a large number of tourists offer greater opportunities for crafters who make items that clearly reflect the local flavor of the community or that are appropriate as souvenirs. If you are located in such an area, consider how you can adapt your products to the tourist market.

If you decide to sell your goods to a retail store, your best bet is to start with a small, independently owned operation where you can deal directly with the owner. Such small-business owners are generally receptive to other small-business owners and suppliers. As you meet more store owners or use the services of an independent sales representative, larger stores may become more accessible and may be willing to take your goods. Larger department store buyers are well aware of the consumer demand for handmade items, and if they think your products will sell, they may place an order for a sizeable lot—anywhere from ten to several hundred—depending on the size of their operation.

Identifying Your Market

As much as you may like to think so, the entire world is not your market. Even producers of major products with widespread appeal, such as soft drinks or affordable consumer electronics, understand that. They can tell you about their customers: how old they are, whether they are male or female, how much money they make, what lifestyle they are likely to enjoy. And you need to be able to do the same thing when it comes to your market.

Candle maker Melony Bell of Fort Meade, Florida, has studied the reasons people buy candles: first, for the scent; second, to create a relaxing ambiance in their homes; and third, for seasonal reasons. "Candles sell to people from 16 up to 50," she says.

Smart Tip

Tip...

Know your competition. Even though you produce one-of-a-kind items, you have competition from other crafters, as well as from the makers of cheaper, mass-produced items sold in many retail stores. Be prepared to compete not only with others exhibitors who sell similar items, but with all the other exhibitors, as well as area retailers who might sell similar merchandise.

It's also important to understand the thought process that goes into the purchase of your products. Are you making inexpensive impulse items? Do customers need to consider issues such as design, color, and size before they make a decision? "Our things are not impulse items, and they won't work in a show where people just want to do impulse buying and are looking for $5 or $6 items," says Jay Norman of his wood pieces, which include small tabletop cabinets with drawers, jewelry boxes, and larger chests.

Market research will provide you with relevant data to help solve or avoid marketing problems. Conducting thorough market surveys is the foundation of any successful business, and yours will be no exception. Strategies such as market segmentation (identifying specific segments within a market) and product differentiation (creating an identity for your products that separates them from your competitors') would be impossible to develop without market research. Chapter 1 in *Start-Up Basics* explains where to find the information you need and how to conduct basic market research.

Danger: Lurking Competitors

When you exhibit in a crafts show, your primary goal is to get customers to spend their money on your products—and certainly the other crafters are competing with you to this end. But there are other competitors for your customers' cash you need to consider. They include:

○ *Admission fees.* Some shows and festivals charge an admission fee. While it's generally modest, it still reduces the amount of cash customers have to spend once they get to your booth.

○ *Parking.* Particularly in downtown areas and at many commercial venues, customers must pay to park—another cost of attending a show that can affect how much they spend on merchandise.

○ *Food concessions.* The sandwiches, beverages, and snacks sold by vendors can put a dent in a family's pocketbook, often forcing them to choose between enjoying their favorite foods at a festival and buying a crafts item from you.

○ *Other events.* Nearby events can increase traffic but mean additional competition for shoppers' dollars.

These competing elements are not always negative. For example, in higher-end shows, admission and parking fees can help weed out browsers from serious buyers. The point is to be aware of everything that can happen at a show that might dilute your prospective customers' purchasing power.

Your market research must reveal:

- Whether there is a market for your product
- If there is a market, what are its demographics
- What is the best way to reach your market
- The best degree of variety in the range of products you will offer
- How much your market is willing to pay for your products

To gain a better picture of the market for crafts, visit local crafts shows or fairs. Certainly you'll want to consider who is exhibiting and what they're selling, but you should also carefully study the people attending the show. Are they primarily women or men? In what age brackets do they fall? Are they looking for gifts or for decorative accessories? Are they actually buying or just browsing? Doll maker Deb Farish of Manchester, Missouri, says she will attend shows she's considering exhibiting in to see the clientele. "I want to see if people are just tire-kickers or if they are actually carrying purchases out," she says. She also checks out the other exhibitors to see how many are selling dolls and what other types of crafts are available.

You can get a fairly accurate picture of the market for crafts in your area by simply observing several shows, but you should also visit retail stores and study demographic data. Once you have completed your market research, you'll be able to develop a marketing plan that will sell your products. To keep your marketing plan up to date, continue researching and studying your market. Use the "Tally Sheet" on page 18 to track current and prospective customers. See Chapter 9 for more on marketing.

Are You on a Mission?

When you're serious about a business, you work hard to develop a mission—that is, you figure out what you're doing, how and where it's being done and who your customers are. Problems can arise, however, when that mission is not clearly articulated into a statement, written down, and communicated to others.

"A mission statement defines what an organization is, why it exists, its reason for being," says Gerald Graham, former dean of the W. Frank Barton School of Business at Wichita State University in Kansas. "Writing it down and communicating it to others creates a sense of commonality and a more coherent approach to what you're trying to do."

Even in a very small company, a written mission statement helps everyone involved see the big picture and keeps them focused on the true goals of the

Bright Idea
Never say no to a customer. When someone asks for something you don't provide, offer an alternative.

business. According to Graham, at a minimum your mission statement should define who your primary customers are, identify the products and services you produce, and describe the geographical location in which you operate. For example, your mission statement might read "To create high-end handmade dolls for collectors who attend shows in the Southeastern United States or buy over the Internet."

A mission statement should be short—usually just one sentence and certainly no more than two. A good idea is to cap it at 100 words. Anything longer than that isn't a mission statement and will probably confuse your employees. See the "Mission Statement Worksheet" on page 20.

Tally Sheet

Market research is a never-ending process. Once you begin exhibiting at shows, keep track of the people who visit your booth. A simple tally sheet will give you the information you need to tailor your product line to your market.

Show _____

Location _____

Day/date _____

Attendees who stopped at your booth:

	Females	Males	With children
under 16			
17–18			
18–34			
35–49			
50–plus			

Of the attendees who stopped at your booth, who made purchases?

	Females	Males	With children
under 16			
17–18			
18–34			
35–49			
50–plus			

Once you have articulated your message, communicate it as often as possible to everyone in the company, along with customers and suppliers. "Post it on the wall, hold meetings to talk about it, and include a reminder of the statement in employee correspondence," says Graham.

Graham says it is more important to adequately communicate the mission statement to employees than to customers. "Sometimes an organization will try to use a mission statement primarily for promotion and, as an aside, use it to help employees identify what business they're in," he says. "That doesn't work very well. The most effective mission statements are developed strictly for internal communication and discussion, and then if something promotional comes out of it, fine." In other words, your mission statement doesn't have to be clever or catchy—just accurate.

Though your mission statement may never win an advertising or creativity award, it can still be a very effective customer relations tool. One idea is to print your mission statement on a page, have every employee sign it, and provide every prospective and new customer with a copy. You can even include it on your brochures and invoices.

Finally, make sure your suppliers know what your mission statement is; it will help them serve you better if they understand what you're all about.

Artist's Statement

Your mission statement describes the mission of the company you create to manufacture and sell your crafts. Along with that, you need an artist's statement—a statement about your work. It describes your philosophy about what you do and its significance to you.

Your artist's statement will help you articulate your own feelings about what you make, as well as function as an important component of your marketing package. You can display it in a show booth, include it with show applications, provide it to the media for publicity purposes and give copies to customers to help them understand what you do.

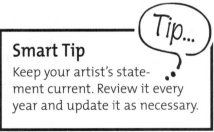

Smart Tip

Keep your artist's statement current. Review it every year and update it as necessary.

Though relatively new to contemporary crafts and art, the artist's statement is directly linked to the selling process. Take some time to think about why you love doing what you do. Use this to educate the public by providing insights into why and how you create your crafts.

The National Association of Independent Artists offers these guidelines for developing your artist's statement:

- Include a photograph of yourself; a portrait is acceptable, but a picture showing you at work is preferred. Be sure you are recognizable.

- Include complete contact information so anyone reading the statement can reach you.
- Identify the medium and processes or techniques you use.
- Identify materials and the methods of handling those materials.
- Include a specific explanation of how your work is produced.
- If you use assistants or apprentices, describe their involvement; if you don't, state that none are used.
- If an outside source such as a foundry or printing lab is used, include that information.
- Do not include resume-type information such as awards, exhibitions, collections, and so on. This information can be included in your biography or resume.
- Other educational information may be included in your artist's statement if you have room.
- Limit the statement to one page, ideally 8 by 11 inches.

If well-known artists have influenced you and your work, name them in your statement. Write in the first person, keep it simple and friendly but passionate, and be honest. Do not use your statement to review your own work—that's for someone else to do. When you've finished your statement, have someone who knows you well read it to be sure it really sounds like you and is easy to comprehend.

Mission Statement Worksheet

To develop an effective mission statement, answer these questions:

1. What products and/or services do we produce? _____
   _____

2. What geographical location do we operate in? _____
   _____

3. Why does my company exist? Whom do we serve? What is our purpose?
   _____
   _____

4. What are our strengths, weaknesses, opportunities, and threats? _____
   _____
   _____

5. Considering the above, along with our expertise and resources, what business should we be in? _____
   _____

6. What is important to us? What do we stand for? _____
   _____

4

Structuring Your Business

There's a lot to do when you start a business. This chapter will address various issues you need to deal with as you get set up. Some of these tasks are more interesting and fun than others, but they are all important and need your attention.

▲

Naming Your Company

One of the most important marketing tools you will ever have is your company's name. A well-chosen name can work very hard for you; an ineffective name means you have to work much harder at marketing your company.

Your company name should very clearly identify what you do in a way that will appeal to your target market. It should be short, catchy, and memorable. It should also be easy to pronounce and spell—people who can't say your company name may buy from you, but they won't refer you to anyone else. Jay and Dianne Norman of DeLand, Florida, make products from wood that help people get organized, so they named their company Organize with Wood. Melony Bell in Fort Meade, Florida, added a clever element when she named her business Luv Shack Candle Co. Deb Farish kept it simple and straightforward with Dolls by Deb, her Manchester, Missouri, company.

Though naming your company is without a doubt a creative process, it helps to take a systematic approach. Once you've decided on a name, or perhaps two or three possibilities, take the following steps:

- *Check the name for effectiveness and ease of use.* Does it quickly and easily convey what you do? Is it easy to say and spell? Is it memorable in a positive way? Ask several of your friends and associates to serve as a focus group to help you evaluate the name's impact.

- *Search for potential conflicts in your local market.* Find out if any other local or regional business serving your market area has a name so similar that yours might confuse the public. Check with your state's division of corporations (or similar agency—your town hall should know where to direct you) to see if someone else has registered the name. If anyone else has, that doesn't preclude you from using the name, but you probably want to avoid it.

- *Check for use on the World Wide Web.* If someone else is already using your name as a domain site on the World Wide Web, consider coming up with something else. Even if you have no intention of developing a Web site of your own, the use could be confusing to your customers.

- *Check to see if the name conflicts with any name listed on your state's trademark register.* Your state department

---

Bright Idea

When you're naming your company, consider creating a word that doesn't exist— that's what companies like Exxon and Kodak did. Just be sure that the syllables blend to make an ear-appealing sound and that the name is simple enough for people to remember and say. Also, make sure you haven't come up with a name that means something in another language.

of commerce can either help you or direct you to the correct agency. You should also check with the trademark register maintained by the U.S. Patent and Trademark Office (PTO), which is listed in the Appendix.

Once the name you've chosen passes these tests, you need to register it as a fictitious business name with the appropriate state agency; again, your state department of commerce (or similar agency) can help you. (Fictitious means only that you're operating a business under a name other than your own.) If you expect to be doing business on a national level—for example, if you'll be handling mail orders or operating on the Internet—you should also register the name with the PTO.

Trademarks and Copyrights

Trademark issues go beyond the name of your company to include the names of the products you'll create. Exactly what is a trademark? According to the PTO, "A trademark includes any word, name, symbol, or device, or any combination, used, or intended to be used, in commerce to identify and distinguish the goods of one manufacturer or seller from goods manufactured or sold by others, and to indicate the source of the goods. In short, a trademark is a brand name."

Registering your trademark is not essential, but it does offer some benefits. It gives notice to the public of your claim of ownership of the mark, a legal presumption of ownership nationwide, and the exclusive right to use the mark on or in connection with the goods or services set forth in the registration.

You can access information about the process of applying for trademark protection and patents on the PTO's Web site.

Once you have established a trademark, you must use it or you risk losing it. Trademarks not actively used for two or more years may be considered abandoned—which means someone else can begin using the mark and you will have no recourse.

You also need to control your mark. Do not allow others to use your mark without your consent, or without restricting what product or service it represents. Think about how companies like McDonald's and Walt Disney Co. aggressively pursue unauthorized use of their trademarks. They understand how much they have to lose if they fail to control their marks.

If you discover someone using your mark without your authorization, consult with an attorney to determine the most appropriate and effective action. By the same token, respect other marks. Just as you don't want anyone infringing on your trademark, don't infringe on others.

Copyrights protect authors of original works once that work is created in a tangible or fixed form. The protection exists immediately at the work's creation. Registration is not required, but it has advantages.

Copyright owners have the right to reproduce the work, to prepare derivative works based on the original work, to distribute copies of the work, and to display the work publicly. In terms of crafts items, copyrightable works include the following categories: pictorial, graphic, and sculptural works.

An idea cannot be copyrighted; copyright law protects only a tangible form of expression. Also, copyright law does not protect titles, names, short phrases, and slogans; familiar symbols or designs; mere variations of typographic ornamentation, lettering, or coloring; mere listings of ingredients or contents.

The use of a copyright notice is no longer required under U.S. law to defend a copyright; however, it is beneficial because it is a clear statement of your claim and ownership. For more information on copyrights, contact the U.S. Copyright Office at the Library of Congress (www.loc.gov/copyright).

Of course, just because you register your work appropriately, you aren't automatically protected from copyright infringement. Some people will copy your work innocently, not realizing that they are violating the law and causing you economic harm. Others do it deliberately because they know most artists aren't inclined to pursue copyright violations. A crafter who makes etched glass doors and windows says he has had people come into his booth at shows with tracing paper and blatantly copy his patterns. Doll maker Deb Farish says she had a woman buy a doll at a show, and as she was paying for it, said she was going to take it apart and make a pattern out of it. "I told her to go ahead. I've seen some people duplicate what I do in other pieces—it's really a compliment. But this is not a cookie-cutter process, and every piece is going to have its own distinguishing look to it. There are some things you can't duplicate, things that are going to be unique to the artist."

If you do decide to take legal action on a copyright violation, typically what you'll do is request injunctive relief, or a judicial order requiring the infringer to stop what he or she is doing. You may also have the infringing articles impounded and disposed of. Your attorney can advise you on whether to pursue damage awards or other financial compensation.

Choosing a Legal Structure

One of the first decisions you'll need to make about your new business is the legal structure of your company. This is an important decision, and it can affect your financial liability, the amount of taxes you pay, and the degree of ultimate control you have over the company. However, legal structure shouldn't be confused with operating structure. Attorney Robert S. Bernstein, managing partner with Bernstein Bernstein Krawec & Wymard, P.C., explains the difference: "The legal structure is the ownership structure—who actually owns the company. The operating structure defines who makes management decisions and runs the company."

Strength in Numbers

Many crafters function as sole proprietors, but find teaming up with other crafters occasionally can be beneficial. For example, if you know someone who uses the same raw materials you do, you can combine your purchasing to take advantage of quantity discounts.

You might also want to share booth space at shows. Doll maker Deb Farish of Dolls by Deb in Manchester, Missouri, does shows with a woman who makes fabric-covered baskets. They met at a show, became friends and now exhibit together. "Her display was very different from mine. She didn't need places for dolls to sit. She hung her baskets on clothes racks. So we could share a space and cut our costs." If you use independent sales reps, you might maximize their efforts by having them represent you and another craftsperson whose products complement yours.

You don't need a full formal partnership to build business relationships that will benefit all involved.

A sole proprietorship is owned by the proprietor, a partnership is owned by the partners, and a corporation is owned by the shareholders. A relatively new business structure is the limited liability company (LLC), which combines the tax advantages of a sole proprietorship with the liability protection of a corporation. The rules on LLCs vary by state; check with your state's department of corporations for the latest requirements.

Sole proprietorships and partnerships can be operated however the owners choose. In a corporation, typically the shareholders elect directors, who in turn elect officers, who then employ other people to run and work in the company. But it's entirely possible for a corporation to have only one shareholder, and to essentially function as a sole proprietorship. In any case, how you plan to operate the company should not be a major factor in your choice of legal structures.

So what goes into choosing a legal structure? The first point, says Bernstein, is who makes the decision on the legal structure. If you're starting the company by yourself, you don't need to take anyone else's preferences into consideration. "But if there are multiple people involved, you need to consider how you're going to relate to each other in the business," he says. "You also need to consider the issue of asset protection and limiting your liability in the event things don't go well."

Something else to think about is your target customers and what their perception will be of your structure. While it's not necessarily true, Bernstein says, "There is a tendency to believe that the legal form of a business has some relationship to the sophistication of the owners, with the sole proprietor as the least and the corporation

▲

> ## Smart Tip
> *Tip...*
>
> Review your business plan once a year. Check to see if you're still on track—if not, do you need to change what you're doing, or change the plan?

as the most sophisticated." He adds that that perception is not necessarily true.

Your image notwithstanding, the biggest advantage of forming a corporation is in the area of asset protection, which, says Bernstein, is the process of making sure that the assets that you don't want to put into the business don't stand liable for the business debt. However, to take advantage of the protection a corporation offers, you must respect the corporation's identity. That means maintaining the corporation as a separate entity; keeping your corporate and personal funds separate, even if you are the sole shareholder; and following your state's rules regarding holding annual meetings and other record-keeping requirements.

Most one-person crafts businesses are sole proprietorships, which are created simply by stating the fact that you are in business. If you opt to set up a corporation, LLC, or partnership, you don't need an attorney. Bernstein says there are plenty of good do-it-yourself books and kits on the market, and most of the state agencies that oversee corporations have guidelines you can use. Even so, it's always a good idea to have a lawyer at least look over your documents before you file them, just to make sure they are complete, and will allow you to function as you want.

Finally, remember that your choice of legal structure is not an irrevocable decision, although if you're going to make a switch, it's easier to go from the simpler forms to the more sophisticated ones than the other way around. Bernstein says the typical pattern is to start as a sole proprietor, then move up to a corporation as the business grows. But if you need the asset protection of a corporation from the beginning, start out that way. Bernstein says, "If you're going to the trouble to start a business, decide on a structure, and put it all together, it's worth the extra effort to make sure it's really going to work." For more information on business legal structures, see Chapter 2 in *Start-Up Basics*.

Licenses and Permits

Most cities and counties require business operators to obtain various licenses and permits to comply with local regulations. While you are still in the planning stages, check with your local planning and zoning department or city/county business license department to find out what licenses and permits you will need and how to obtain them. You may need some or all of the following:

- *Occupational license or permit.* This is typically required by the city (or county if you are not within an incorporated city) for just about every business operating within its jurisdiction. License fees are essentially a tax, and the rates vary widely based on the location and type of business. As part of the application process, the licensing bureau will check to make sure there are no zoning restrictions prohibiting you from operating. This is particularly important if you are going to be using chemicals or operating equipment that could be noisy.

- *Fire department permit.* If your business is open to the public, you may be required to have a permit from the local fire department.

- *Sign permit.* Many cities and suburbs have sign ordinances that restrict the size, location, and sometimes the lighting and type of sign you can use in front of your business. Landlords may also impose their own restrictions. Most residential areas forbid signs altogether. To avoid costly mistakes, check regulations, and secure the written approval of your landlord before you invest in a sign.

- *State licenses.* Many states require persons engaged in certain occupations to hold licenses or occupational permits. Often, these people must pass state examinations before they can conduct business. States commonly require licensing for auto mechanics, plumbers, electricians, building contractors, collection agents, insurance agents, real estate brokers, repossessors, and personal service providers such as doctors, nurses, barbers, cosmetologists, etc. It is highly unlikely that you will need a state license to operate your crafts business, but it's a good idea to check with your state's occupation licensing entity to be sure.

In addition to basic business licenses, you may need some special licenses depending on what you make and where you live. For example, crafter Anita Fetter says the state of Ohio requires her to have a vendor's license, a stuffing license, and a batting license, which assures that her stuffed animals and quilted crafts are made with new, safe materials and not used or recycled goods. Your state department of commerce should be able to give you the information you need on these types of licenses, or direct you to the proper agency.

Sales Tax Number

When you sell at retail, you are responsible for collecting and remitting sales tax to the appropriate government agencies. To do this, you must have a sales tax ID number, also known as a sellers permit or resale permit, issued by your state.

▲

Agencies issuing these permits vary with each state, but generally they are the Department of Revenue, the State Sales Tax Commission, or the Franchise Tax Board. Contact the entity responsible for governing taxes in your state to find out how to apply for your sales tax number.

This permit allows you to avoid putting out money for sales tax on materials at the time you purchase them from suppliers. You're able to defer remitting the taxes on your finished items until you sell them.

Business Insurance

It takes a lot to start a business, even a small one, so protect your investment with adequate insurance. If you're homebased, don't assume your homeowners or renters policy covers your business equipment—chances are, it doesn't. If you're located in a commercial facility, be prepared for your landlord to require proof of certain levels of liability insurance when you sign the lease. And in either case, you need coverage for your inventory and other valuables.

A smart approach to insurance is to find an agent who works with businesses similar to yours. The agent should be willing to help you analyze your needs, evaluate what risks you're willing to accept, and what risks you need to insure against, and work with you to keep your insurance costs down.

Typically, homebased crafters will want to make sure their equipment and inventory are protected against theft and damage by a covered peril, such as fire or flood; and that they have some liability protection if someone (either a customer or an employee) is injured on their property or by their product. In most cases, one of the new insurance products designed for homebased businesses will provide sufficient coverage. Also, if you use your vehicle for business, be sure it is adequately covered.

If you opt for a commercial location, you'll find your landlord will probably require certain levels of general liability coverage as part of the terms of your lease. You'll also want to cover your inventory, equipment, and fixtures. Once your business is up and running, consider business interruption insurance to replace lost revenue and pay related costs if you are ever unable to operate due to covered circumstances. For more on business insurance, check out Chapter 7 in *Start-Up Basics*.

Smart Tip

Tip...

Sit down with your insurance agent on an annual basis and review your insurance needs. As your company grows, they are sure to change. Also, insurance companies are always developing new products to meet the needs of the growing small-business market, and it's possible one of these new policies will be more appropriate for you.

Professional Advisors

As a business owner, you may be the boss, but you can't be expected to know everything. You'll occasionally need to turn to professionals for information and assistance. It's a good idea to establish relationships with these professionals before you get into a crisis situation.

To shop for a professional service provider, ask friends and associates for recommendations. You might also check with your local chamber of commerce or trade association for referrals. Find someone who understands your industry and specific business and appears eager to work with you. Check them out with the Better Business Bureau and the appropriate state licensing agency before committing yourself.

As a crafts business owner, the professional service providers you're likely to need include:

- *Attorney.* You need a lawyer who practices in the area of business law, is honest and appreciates your patronage. In most parts of the United States, there are many lawyers willing to compete fiercely for the privilege of serving you. Interview several and choose one you feel comfortable with. Be sure to clarify the fee schedule ahead of time, and get your agreement in writing. Keep in mind that good commercial lawyers don't come cheap; if you want good advice, you must be willing to pay for it. Your attorney should review all contracts, leases, letters of intent, and other legal documents before you sign them. You may want to discuss product liability issues with your attorney. He or she can also help you collect bad debts and establish personnel policies and procedures for the time when you want to hire employees. Of course, if you are unsure of the legal ramifications of any situation, call your attorney immediately.

- *Accountant.* Among your outside advisors, your accountant is likely to have the greatest impact on the success or failure of your business. If you are forming a corporation, your accountant should counsel you on tax issues during start-up. On an ongoing basis, your accountant can help you organize the statistical data concerning your business, assist in charting future actions based on past performance, and advise you on your overall financial strategy regarding purchasing, capital investment, and other matters related to your business goals. A good accountant will also serve as a tax advisor, making sure that you are in compliance with all applicable regulations and that you don't overpay any taxes.

> ## Bright Idea
> Check with your local economic development agency for start-up guidance. Most of these agencies have a range of assistance programs to help new businesses get started (since it's good for the local economy).

- *Insurance agent.* A good independent insurance agent can assist you with all aspects of your business insurance, from general liability to employee benefits, and probably even handle your personal lines as well. Look for an agent who works with a wide range of insurers and understands the crafts industry in general and your business in particular. This agent should be willing to explain the details of various types of coverage, consult with you to determine the most appropriate cover-

age, help you understand the degree of risk you are taking, work with you in developing risk-reduction programs, and assist in expediting any claims.

- *Banker.* You need a business bank account and a relationship with a banker. Don't just choose the bank you've always done your personal banking with; it may not be the best bank for your business. Interview several bankers before making a decision on where to place your business. Once your account is opened, maintain a relationship with the banker. Periodically sit down and review your accounts and the services you use to make sure you are getting the package most appropriate for your situation. Ask for advice if you have financial questions or problems. When you need a loan or a bank reference to provide to creditors, the relationship you've established will work in your favor.

- *Consultants.* The consulting industry is booming, and for good reason. Consultants can provide valuable, objective input on all aspects of your business. Consider hiring a business consultant to evaluate your business plan or a marketing consultant to assist you in that area. When you are ready to hire employees, a human resources consultant may help you avoid some costly mistakes. Consulting fees vary widely, depending on the individual's experience, location, and field of expertise. If you can't afford to hire a consultant, consider contacting the business school at the nearest college or university and hiring an MBA student to help you.

- *Computer expert.* You'll use a computer to manage your business and may even use computers in the design and creation of your products. Your computer and data are extremely valuable assets, so if you don't know much about computers, find someone to help you select a system and the appropriate software, and to be available to help you maintain, troubleshoot, and expand your system as you need it.

Shipping and Receiving

Dollar Stretcher

Don't pay for more for freight service than you need. Most over- night companies offer two or three levels of next-day service—early mornings, before noon, and afternoon. The earlier the delivery, the higher the cost. If next afternoon will meet your customer's needs, don't pay for morning delivery. And if the carrier misses the delivery time, insist it honor its guarantee by refunding the charges.

Most crafts businesses have to deal with shipping and receiving on a regular basis, both to send finished products out and to receive inventory and supplies. Your volume and service needs will dictate what carriers you choose, so do your homework before making a final decision. And while you may be more aware of national carriers such as the U.S. Postal Service, UPS, and FedEx, don't overlook the idea of local delivery services and regional freight carriers. Many of these carriers offer competitive rates and are hungry for your business. Shop around for the best price/service package.

Freight is an important part of your business, both from a price and service standpoint. The cost of freight is a direct expense

The Hidden Profit-Eater

Freight is a variable expense that can be hard to predict but has a definite—and often significant—impact on your bottom line. As you shop for and build relationships with suppliers, consider where they are located and how much it will cost for you to receive their goods.

Track your freight costs carefully, and be sure each charge is accurate. It's a good idea to check periodically to make sure the weight of the shipment matches the weight you were charged for. And if your supplier prepays the freight charges and adds it to your merchandise invoice, verify that the rates have been correctly calculated.

If you buy primarily from local suppliers and pick up the merchandise yourself, you still need to consider the cost of getting the material from their location to yours. In this situation, your time and vehicle expenses need to be considered as "freight costs" when you're calculating a fair and reasonable markup for the goods.

that affects your bottom line and needs to be calculated into your pricing. And when the freight company makes a mistake, is late with a delivery, or loses or damages a package, it could adversely affect your relationship with your customers. So choose your freight companies carefully and demand that they perform up to your high standards.

Keeping the
Cash Flowing

Most of the crafters we talked with for this book started their businesses with the equipment they had accumulated when they did their craft as a hobby, so they considered their start-up costs to be minimal. The cost of the equipment they had varied significantly, depending on the type of craft involved.

Jay Norman of Organize with Wood in DeLand, Florida, had been accumulating woodworking tools all his life. "It was more evolutionary rather than one lump sum of cash," he says. Of course, for wood products—especially larger ones—the raw materials tend to be more expensive than for many other crafts. In the beginning, Jay and his wife, Dianne, used the sales from one show to buy supplies to replenish their inventory for the next show. "You can start with just inventory for one show and keep reinvesting," Dianne says.

Dollar Stretcher

You may be able to reduce your tax liability by deducting the cost of equipment you already owned when you started your business. Talk to your accountant or tax advisor about this.

Judy Infinger, who runs her business, Wood and Threads, out of Altamonte Springs, Florida, also already owned woodworking equipment, so her start-up costs consisted primarily of getting her sales tax number and establishing her business name. By the time Gladys Johnson in Bunn, North Carolina, decided to start selling her porcelain dolls through her business Dolls by Gladys, she had already purchased the equipment she needed as a hobbyist. "It's not an inexpensive hobby to begin with," she notes. "If you get a kiln, you can expect to pay $1,000 or more. Molds range anywhere from $150 to $400."

Manchester, Missouri's Deb Farish says the start-up costs for her business, Dolls by Deb, were nominal and consisted of purchasing fabric and other doll-making supplies. "I got a credit card so I could take advantage of buying bulk quantities of muslin, stuffing, and items I used the most of," she says. "That way I could conserve my cash for paying for show registrations."

It cost Lynn Korff about $500 to get her Web site set up for Korff Ceramic Originals. She already owned her equipment from her ceramics shop, so her investment in her current business was minimal. Melony Bell borrowed $500 from her husband's business to start her candle-making operation in Fort Meade, Florida. She quickly paid that back and continued to build her company by reinvesting profits. Her low start-up costs were due primarily to the fact that she had already purchased equipment to use as a hobby. If you are starting from scratch, she estimates that it would take between $8,000 and $10,000 to buy wax melters, wax, and oils in bulk, and other necessary supplies.

No matter what kind of equipment you already own, once you go from hobbyist to business person, there are some items you will need to buy. For example, if you are going to sell at crafts shows, you'll need tags, business cards, brochures, bags, wrapping materials, etc. You'll also need to get your crafts, supplies, and booth equipment to and from the shows, and that could mean buying a new vehicle and/or a trailer. If you are going to sell via the Internet, by special order or by mail order, you'll need shipping materials (boxes, packing materials, tape, labels, etc.). In any case, you'll need administrative and bookkeeping items such as invoices, receipts, credit card processing equipment, record-keeping software, and supplies. So where do you get the money to buy all these things before you start selling your crafts?

Sources of Start-Up Funds

As you're putting together your financial plan, consider these sources of start-up funds:

- *Your own resources.* Do a thorough inventory of your assets. People generally have more assets than they immediately realize. This could include savings accounts, equity in real estate, retirement accounts, vehicles, recreation equipment, collections, and other investments. You may opt to sell assets for cash or use them as collateral for a loan. Take a look, too, at your personal line of credit; most of the equipment and supplies you'll need are available through retail stores that accept credit cards.

- *Friends and family.* The logical next step after gathering your own resources is to approach friends and relatives who believe in you and want to help you succeed. Be cautious with these arrangements; no matter how close you are, present yourself professionally, put everything in writing, and be sure the individuals you approach can afford to take the risk of investing in your business.

Smart Tip *Tip...*
Before asking friends or relatives for a loan, show them your business plan and ask for a critique. Their input will give you a better idea of how receptive they may be to lending you money or investing in your company.

- *Partners.* Though most crafts businesses are owned by just one person, you may want to consider using the "strength in numbers" principle and look around for someone who may want to team up with you in your venture. You may choose someone who has financial resources and wants to work side by side with you in the business. Or you may find someone who has money to invest but no interest in doing the actual work. Be sure to create a written partnership agreement that clearly defines your respective rights, responsibilities, and obligations.

- *Government programs.* Take advantage of the abundance of local, state and federal programs designed to support small businesses in general. Make your first stop the SBA then investigate various other programs. Women, minorities, and veterans should check out niche financing possibilities designed to help these groups get into business. The business section of your local library is a good place to begin your research.

Learn more about financing a new business in Chapter 4 in *Start-Up Basics.*

Pricing Your Handcrafted Items

Another critical financial issue is deciding how much to charge for your products. Pricing can be tedious and time-consuming, especially if you don't have a knack for juggling numbers. If your prices are too low, you rob yourself of profits, or are forced to reduce the quality of your product to maintain your profitability. If your prices are too high, you may lose business. In fact, many craftspeople are afraid that if they price their goods at what they're worth, no one will buy them.

When you're pricing an item, you need to consider the cost of the materials used to make it, freight charges (if any), the cost of your labor, a proportionate share of your overhead (including fixed and variable operating expenses), and a reasonable profit. After computing all of these factors, your price may seem unreasonable to some customers. At that point, you need to decide whether you're going to stick with that number or figure out a way to reduce the price and still make a fair profit.

Many crafters feel they are never truly compensated for their labor, but because they love what they do, they're willing to accept that.

"You never get what you deserve for the hours you put in," says Dianne. "We're not becoming rich doing this; we're doing this because it's what we love."

Deb agrees: "You don't get rich financially, but there are other rewards. This is a labor of love that we make money at."

"I don't charge enough for my time, but you have to be practical," says Lynn. "If I charged $60 per piggy bank, I wouldn't sell any."

After reading this section on pricing, visit several crafts shows and check the prices of items similar to those you intend to sell. Ask the crafters who made them how their products are selling. After visiting several exhibits, you should have a pretty good idea of the general market price for what you want to make. Compare that with the price you developed using your costs-plus-profit formula. If your items are more expensive, can you reduce your materials cost or figure out how to make your production more efficient to reduce your labor cost? Or, are the materials and workmanship in your products of higher quality? If so, be sure your customers realize that.

Other questions to ask yourself include:

- Could I save money by purchasing materials from a discount crafts supplier instead of a local crafts store?

> **Bright idea**
>
> When you're pricing items for sale at a crafts show, consider including the sales tax in the marked price and rounding off to the nearest dollar. Doll maker Deb Farish says it makes the entire process cleaner and easier; you don't have to calculate tax during the show or make change for odd amounts.

Cheaper by the Dozen

When you're getting started, you're probably thinking of pricing only in terms of retail. This can create some challenges if you decide to get into wholesaling later on. Wholesale customers—typically retail stores that are going to resell your products—generally double the wholesale price to arrive at the retail price they charge their customers. For example, if they pay $10 for an item, they'll sell it for $20.

To develop a wholesale price list, you must first determine a reasonable retail price for your products. Then decide if you have the resources to produce the items in quantity, recover your expenses, and still make a profit if you sell the items for half of their retail price. Your wholesale price must reflect the actual costs of production.

- Could I move into another studio with lower rent and reduce my overhead?
- Is the retail store owner's or sales rep's commission too high?
- Do I spend too long on perfecting every detail when I'm making my goods?

Examine every factor in your formula and decide how you can reduce the costs of making your products.

Keep in mind that such factors as high overheads (particularly when you're renting a retail store), unpredictable insurance rates, shrinkage (shoplifting, employee, or other theft), seasonality, shifts in wholesale product costs and freight expenses, and sales or discounts will all affect the final pricing.

Other factors that can influence your final price include:

- *Delivery/shipping.* If you sell on the Internet or by mail order, or if people don't want to carry your product around at a crafts show, you'll have to deal with shipping charges. Decide if this will be an add-on or included in the basic price.
- *Credit terms.* When you sell at wholesale, your credit terms can be part of your pricing structure. Consider offering a discount for early payment to improve your cash flow.
- *Returns policy.* Under what circumstances will you take products back and how will that affect your operating costs?
- *Packaging.* What will it cost you to provide sufficient packaging so the customer can get the item home in good condition?

▲

Doing the Calculations

To arrive at a strong pricing structure for your particular crafts business, consider these three factors: labor and materials (or supplies), overhead, and profit.

1. *Labor and materials.* Until you establish records to use as a guide, you'll have to estimate the costs of labor and materials. Labor costs include wages and benefits you pay yourself and employees if you have them. Labor cost is usually expressed as an hourly rate.

2. *Overhead.* Overhead consists of all the nonlabor, indirect expenses required to operate your business. Your overhead rate is usually calculated as a percentage of your labor and materials. If you have past operating expenses to guide you, figuring an overhead rate is not difficult. Total your expenses for one year, excluding labor and materials. Divide this number by your total cost of labor and materials to determine your overhead rate. When you're starting out, you won't have past expenses to guide you, so you'll have to estimate. You can raise or lower the numbers later to suit the realities of your operation.

3. *Profit.* Profit is, of course, the difference between what it costs you to make and deliver a product and what you charge the customer. Figure your net profit into your price by applying a markup percentage to the combined costs of labor, materials, and overhead. The markup percentage will be larger than the actual percentage of gross revenue you'll end up with for your net profit. For example, if you plan to net 38 percent before taxes out of your gross revenue, you will need to apply a markup percentage of about 61.3 to your labor and materials plus overhead to achieve that target.

People often confuse markup and gross profit on a single product or group of products. When expressed as percentages, gross profit is always figured as a percentage of the selling *price*, while markup is traditionally figured as a percentage of the seller's *cost*.

To learn more about pricing, see Chapter 16 in *Start-Up Basics.*

What Crafters Charge

While it's highly recommended that you work through the pricing exercises described above, the reality is that many crafters just don't want to do that. They feel that charging for their actual time drives their prices up too high, or they have figured out another formula that works for them.

Jay and Dianne have found that simply tripling the cost of the raw materials to reach their retail price works well for them and their customer base. Deb uses a similar formula in pricing her dolls. Of her retail price, a third is for costs (materials and labor), a third is for the costs of marketing and selling (primarily entering shows), and a third is profit. That formula keeps her dolls priced competitively. Gladys' porcelain

Calculating Markup

Unless you're a mathematics whiz, you may find calculating markup confusing. The following table shows you the percentage you need to mark up your operating costs to reach the desired net profit. Here's how it works: Choose the desired net profit from the left-hand column, then use the markup percent from the corresponding column on the right. For example, if you want a net profit of 4.8 percent, you need to use a markup of 5.01 percent.

Net Profit Percent	Markup Percent	Net Profit Percent Cont.	Markup Percent Cont.	Net Profit Percent Cont.	Markup Percent Cont.
4.8	5.01	22.5	29.0	41.0	70.0
5.0	5.3	23.0	29.9	42.0	72.4
6.0	6.4	23.1	30.0	42.8	75.0
7.0	7.5	24.0	31.6	44.4	80.0
8.0	8.7	25.0	33.3	46.1	85.0
9.0	10.0	26.0	35.0	47.5	90.0
10.0	11.1	27.0	37.0	50.0	100
10.7	12.0	27.3	37.5	52.4	110
11.0	12.4	28.0	39.0	54.5	120
11.1	12.5	28.5	40.0	56.5	130
12.0	13.6	29.0	40.9	58.3	140
12.5	14.3	30.0	42.9	60.0	150
13.0	15.0	32.0	47.1	61.5	160
14.0	16.3	33.3	50.0	63.0	170
15.0	17.7	34.0	51.5	64.2	180
16.0	19.1	35.0	53.9	65.5	190
16.7	20.0	35.5	55.0	66.7	200
17.0	20.5	36.0	56.3	69.2	225
18.0	22.0	37.0	58.8	71.4	250
18.5	22.7	37.5	60.0	73.3	275
19.0	23.5	38.0	~.3	75.0	300
20.0	25.0	39.0	64.0	76.4	325
21.0	26.6	39.5	65.5	77.8	350
22.0	28.2	40.0	66.7	78.9	375

dolls range from $100 to $600, depending on the materials. She doesn't use a formula to price, but relies on her knowledge of what the market will bear.

To price her ceramics, Lynn calculates the cost of materials and firing, then adds 50 percent plus shipping to reach her final retail cost. Including the shipping expense in her retail price allows her to promote her terms as including "free shipping"; it's also easier for the customer to calculate the final price.

Dollar Stretcher

Many shipping companies (the U.S. Postal Service, FedEx, UPS, and others) provide their customers with free shipping boxes. Using this benefit can save you a substantial amount in packaging supplies.

Locating and Setting Up

As a crafter, chances are you can work out of your home when you begin. Most part-time crafters who sew, crochet, carve wood, or do similar work already have work spaces set up in their homes before they start their businesses. Some types of crafts allow you to work in your favorite chair while watching television while others require a special work station. Some crafts require very little space and equipment, yet others demand a sizeable work area and special equipment.

If you do not have enough space at home, or if you cannot legally pursue your craft in your home because of zoning or other restrictions, you will need to rent space. Most craftspeople who conduct their business at a commercial facility either rent a studio or a section of a retail store. Studios may be in any type of neighborhood; for example, ceramists often work from studios located in industrial areas. This type of commercial space typically costs less than commercial office or retail space. Your studio should have adequate room for your equipment, supplies, and inventory of finished product, as well as an office for administrative functions.

Let's take a look at the different types of facilities you might use to make and sell your handcrafted items.

Working from Home

The major benefit of starting a homebased business is that it significantly reduces the amount of start-up and initial operating capital you'll need. But there's more to consider than simply the upfront cash. Do you have a separate room for your work area, or will you have to work at the dining room table? Can you set up a comfortable workstation with all the tools and equipment you'll need? Can you separate your work area from the rest of the house so you can have privacy when you're working and get away from "the office" when you're not?

Converting a spare bedroom or den into an office and work area provides the best homebased operation. If this isn't possible, a corner of the garage, basement, or even the kitchen will suffice. Of course, if you require a great deal of space, or if your particular craft creates a mess, you might want to devote your basement, garage, or an outdoor shed—rather than a carpeted room—to your business.

A corner of the workroom can serve as your office, housing your computer, filing system, phone, etc. You will also need storage space to hold your supplies and your finished

> **Tip...**
>
> **Smart Tip**
>
> To take full advantage of the tax breaks available to homebased businesses, you must choose a room—not just the corner of a room—to be used solely as an office or production area. If the room is also used for personal purposes, the IRS may disallow your deduction.

inventory. Depending on what kind of home you have, your garage can be ideal for this purpose. If you don't have enough garage space, a spare room with shelves and a good-sized closet might work well. See next page for sample layouts of an office and a ceramist's studio.

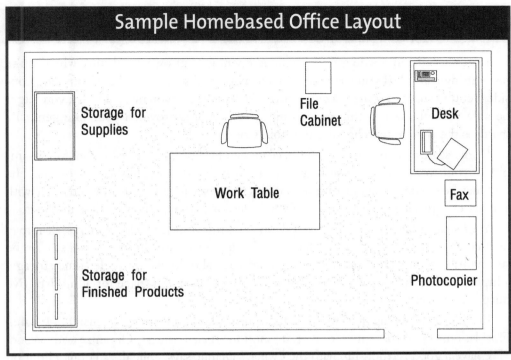

Sample Homebased Office Layout

Storage for Supplies

File Cabinet

Desk

Work Table

Fax

Storage for Finished Products

Photocopier

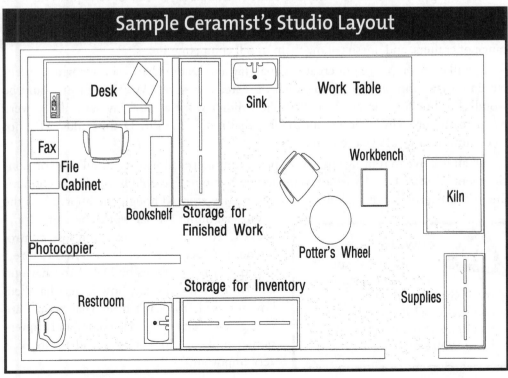

Sample Ceramist's Studio Layout

Desk

Sink

Work Table

Fax

File Cabinet

Workbench

Kiln

Bookshelf

Storage for Finished Work

Photocopier

Potter's Wheel

Restroom

Storage for Inventory

Supplies

Retail Store Space

Experienced crafters do not recommend opening your own retail store when you're just getting started. If you want to sell your merchandise in a retail environment, consider renting space in someone else's store. For example, if you make jewelry, you might be able to rent space within an existing jewelry store, provided your line generally matches the type of merchandise the store stocks.

Before store owners agree to rent space in their facilities, they usually want to see samples of your work and may also require you to have a list of established customers. The rent may be structured in one of several different ways: a flat monthly rate, a flat rate with a utility charge added, a percentage of your sales, or a combination of these methods.

Your space may be dedicated strictly to retailing your finished products, or it may be a combined retail and studio facility. If you plan to use the space as a studio, be sure you have an adequate work area. The space should also provide some storage, a highly visible display of your crafts, security, and as much space for administrative purposes as you require.

In addition to selling their wood crafts at shows, Jay and Dianne Norman of DeLand, Florida, rent retail space in a local crafts shop for their business, Organize with Wood. "We have a good relationship with the owner," Dianne says. "She doesn't put a limit on what we can bring, so we can try whatever we think will sell. And she makes suggestions to us based on what customers are asking for." The store owner rents space to a wide range of crafters, and doesn't allow them to sell competing items.

But all craft shops are not created equal. Jay and Dianne had a similar arrangement with another shop in a larger town with greater exposure. "We thought it would be wonderful, but for our product, that shop didn't work at all," Jay says. They were never really sure why it didn't, but the fact that it didn't is why Dianne adds, "Try not to commit to a whole year contract."

An alternative to renting space is to place your merchandise in a retail shop on consignment. Crafter Deb Farish of Manchester, Missouri, has sold her dolls on consignment in a nearby beauty salon and a convenience store. Though she appreciates the additional outlet for her work, there are drawbacks to consignment sales. "You lose control of your product when you leave it in the store," says the owner of Dolls by Deb. "You have no control over the display, how it gets handled, how it's used. You can't hear what people are saying, you can't tell what colors and expressions people are looking for, and feedback is very important."

Beware!
In any rental, sublease, or consignment situation, read your contract carefully, and be sure you understand everything before you sign it.

Moving Up and Out

Most crafters start working from their homes to keep costs down, but many eventually run out of space and need to shift to a commercial site. If your business is taking over your home, it may be time to consider moving out.

Consider all your options and costs carefully before making a final decision. You may find the most efficient tactic is to continue working from home but rent storage space for your inventory and supplies. Or you may find that your best bet is to get out of the house completely—and then you have to decide whether you want your own studio or store, or if subleasing a portion of someone else's facility is best. For example, crafter Melony Bell started making her candles at home in Fort Meade, Florida, but she says, "It just got to be too much." Her father-in-law owns a typewriter repair business, and offered her some space in the back of his shop; that arrangement worked well for her particular operation.

Melony Bell in Fort Meade, Florida, found that, having a full-time job in addition to her candle business, made consignments problematic. "It's hard for me to go to the store, make sure they have enough candles, check the display, that sort of thing," she says. Instead, she decided to wholesale candles to several local and regional retailers. To qualify for wholesale prices, the store must buy 12 or more of a particular style of candle. See Chapter 9 for more on consignment sales.

Carts and Kiosks

An alternative to a traditional retail store is a cart or kiosk in a mall. Carts and kiosks are a great way to test your business before moving into a regular store—or you can use them seasonally, during the Christmas shopping rush or any time of year that suits your craft. If you make and sell kites, for example, you could set up your cart in a local mall during the summer and work out of your home the remainder of the year. In addition, if you have a retail store, a temporary cart at another location can generate immediate sales and serve as a marketing tool for your year-round location.

Renting cart or kiosk space is usually significantly less than the rent for an in-line (traditional) store, but rates vary dramatically depending on the location and season. For example, rent in a class C mall during an off-peak season may cost as little as $400 per month for cart space, but a class A mall in December might charge $4,000 to $5,000 per month for the same amount of space.

Carts can be leased or purchased. New carts can be purchased for $3,000 to $5,000; monthly lease fees typically run 8 to 12 percent of the new price. You can probably get a good deal on a used cart; just be sure it suits your needs. If a used cart needs significant modifications to work for you, it may be better to buy new and get exactly what you need. Be sure the cart provides an adequate display for your merchandise and has sufficient storage for at least a full day's inventory—you can restock nightly if necessary.

Though kiosks are often occupied by temporary tenants, they have a greater sense of permanence than carts. They typically offer more space and design flexibility. They're also more expensive—expect to pay $9,000 to $10,000 or more to purchase a new kiosk. As with carts, you may be able to lease a kiosk, although there are not as many available, or you can buy a used kiosk.

Carts and kiosks are available from a variety of sources. Manufacturers and brokers advertise in a variety of retail trade publications (see the Appendix). But before you invest in a cart or kiosk, decide where you're going to put it. Many malls have restrictions on the size and design of temporary tenant facilities; they may also want all such fixtures to look alike.

Freestanding Buildings

If you produce, exhibit, and sell your goods in the same facility and depend on customer visits, you'll need space in a retail area. You may want to consider working from a freestanding building located in a crafter's marketplace or a retail business area, either when you are starting or after you are established. Locating your store at a high-traffic site outside a shopping center or mall also works nicely; you'll pay a lower fixed rent than the mall stores and benefit from the traffic they generate. However, the freestanding store merchant loses the shared (and thus lower) expenses for utilities, pest control, security, trash service, maintenance, and advertising.

If you won't be relying on customers visiting your facility, consider locating in an industrial area. You can use your facility as a studio and sell your products elsewhere (at crafts shows, through the mail, online, to retailers, etc.).

Choosing a Location

Before you actually start shopping for space, you need to have a clear picture of what you *must* have, what you'd *like* to have, what you absolutely won't tolerate—and how much you're able to pay. Developing that picture can be a time-consuming process that is both exciting and tedious, but it's essential that you give it the attention it deserves.

Once you know what you want, start looking around. Keep these points in mind as you shop:

- Are there any ordinances or zoning restrictions that could affect your business in any way? Check this out for neighboring properties as well as for the specific location you're considering—you probably don't want an adult entertainment store opening up next to your crafts business.

- Be sure the building has adequate electrical, air conditioning, and telecommunications service to meet your present and future needs. It's a good idea to hire an independent engineer to check this out for you.

- Are utilities included in the rent? If not, ask the utility companies for summaries of the previous year's usage and billing for the site. Also, find out what the various utility

Beware!

Be wary of incentives. Incentives—such as free rent or tax breaks—often mask serious problems. There's usually a good reason any location offers incentives, and you need to know what it is before you sign up.

providers require in the way of security deposits so you can consider it in your move-in budget.

Commercial Leases

If you've never rented commercial space before, your first glimpse of a commercial lease may be overwhelming. They are lengthy, full of jargon and unfamiliar terms, and always written to the landlord's advantage. But they are negotiable. The key to successful lease negotiations is knowing what you want, understanding what the lease document says, and being reasonable in your demands.

Especially for retail space, be sure your lease includes a bail-out clause, which lets you out of the lease if your sales don't reach an agreed-on amount, and a co-tenancy clause so you can break the lease if an anchor store closes or moves. If you're going to have to do a substantial amount of work to get the space ready for occupancy, consider negotiating a construction allowance—generally $5 to $25 per square foot—to help offset the costs.

Be sure you clearly understand what is *rentable* and what is *usable* space. Rentable space is what you pay for; usable is what you can actually use to run your business; typically it doesn't include hallways, restrooms, lobbies, elevator shafts, stairwells, etc.

You may be expected to pay a prorated portion of common area maintenance costs. This is not unusual, but be sure that the fees are reasonable and that the landlord isn't making a profit on this function. Also, check for clauses that allow the landlord the right to remodel at the tenants' expense without prior approval and insist on language that limits your financial liability.

Negotiating the Lease

The first lease the landlord presents is usually just the starting point. You may be surprised at what you can get in the way of concessions and extras simply by asking.

Different Strokes

If you rent space for your business, you should be aware that there are several types of leases:

○ *Flat lease.* The oldest and simplest form of lease, the flat lease sets a single price for a definite period of time. It generally is the best deal for the tenant, but is becoming increasingly harder to find. Caution: Avoid a flat lease if the term is too short; a series of short-term flat leases could cost you more in the long run than a longer-term lease with reasonable escalation clauses.

○ *Step lease.* The step lease attempts to cover the landlord's expected increases in expenses by increasing the monthly rental on an annual basis over the life of the agreement. The problem with step leases is that they are based on estimates rather than actual costs, and there's no way for either party to be sure in advance that the proposed increases are fair and equitable.

○ *Net lease.* Similar to a step lease, the net lease increases the rent to cover increases in the landlord's costs, but does so on the exact increases when they occur rather than on estimates. This may be more equitable than a step lease, but it's less predictable.

○ *Cost of living lease.* Rather than tying rent increases to specific expenses, this type of lease bases increases on the Cost of Living index. Your rent will go up with general inflation.

○ *Percentage lease.* This lease lets the landlord benefit from your success. The rent is based on either a minimum or base amount, or a percentage of your business's gross revenue, whichever is higher. Percentages typically range from 3 to 12 percent. With this type of lease, you'll be required to periodically furnish proof of gross sales; to do this, you may allow the landlord to examine your books or sales tax records, or provide a copy of the appropriate section of your tax return. Percentage leases are especially common for retail space.

Of course, you need to be reasonable and keep your demands in line with acceptable business practices and current market conditions. A good commercial real estate agent can be invaluable with this. Avoid issuing ultimatums; they almost always close doors—and if you fail to follow through, your next "ultimatum" won't mean much. Consider beginning the process with something that's close to your "best and final offer"—that way, your negotiations won't be lengthy and protracted, and you can either reach a mutually acceptable deal or move on to a different property. The longer negotiations take, the more potential there is for things to go wrong.

Essentially, everything in the lease is subject to negotiation, including economic terms, rent commencement and escalation, tenant leasehold improvements, options, tenant's rights and exposures, and other general terms and conditions. You or your agent can negotiate the lease, but then it should be drawn up by an attorney. Typically, the landlord or the landlord's attorney will draft the lease, and an attorney you hire who specializes in real estate should review it for you before you sign.

Buying an Existing Operation

Taking over an existing craftsperson's facility or a similar operation often seems like a simple shortcut for prospective owners. Advertisements of stores for sale can be found through trade publications, shopping center publications, local newspapers, and rental agents.

Retailers frequently purchase shops "lock, stock, and barrel," including store fixtures and equipment, inventory, and office and store supplies. This type of arrangement would be appropriate for a ceramist, jeweler, wood-carver, or even a glass artist. Some craftspeople, however, prefer to buy the fixtures, equipment, and leasehold improvements and remain free to create their own inventory and image. Purchasing an entire facility, including existing inventory and supplies, can cost up to hundreds of thousands of dollars.

A buyer can go astray, however, by selecting a store that is already doomed, perhaps by a poor location or the unfavorable reputation of the former owner. Neighborhood merchants can often provide useful information about business conditions in the area. Before buying an existing business, take the following steps:

- Investigate why the store is for sale. Is the location suitable for your crafts business? Has damaging competition moved in?

- Examine the store's financial records for the last three years and for the current year-to-date. Compare store sales tax records with the owner's claims.

- Sit in on the store's operation for a few days, observing daily business volume and clientele.

- Evaluate the worth of existing store fixtures. These fixtures must be in good condition and consistent with your plans for store image and merchandise. Fixtures may include a work bench and the surrounding work area.

- Determine the costs of remodeling and redecorating if you will be changing the store's decor. Will these costs negate the advantage of buying?

- Decide what existing inventory might suit your store plan and could be included in the purchase. Most sellers deplete their inventory to lower the store's price. Even so, any undesirable stock is a waste of the buyer's money.

▲

Craft Shows and Fairs

Most crafters begin the retail side of their business by exhibiting at shows and crafts malls. Craft shows originated as summertime outdoor events in rural areas as an outlet for part-time craftspeople to sell their goods. In the late 1970s, show organizers began holding events indoors, which meant they could be staged year-round. In addition, organizers recognized a market for crafts shows in urban areas. Crafts show vendors include craftspeople who exhibit and sell their handmade goods, as well as suppliers who market their products to craftspeople and the general public.

Community crafts fairs or bazaars typically take place during the summer months, when vendors can set up outside. Of course, in mild and moderate climates, you'll see outdoor shows in the spring and fall, and sometimes even during the winter months. These events are held on weekends, and typically last one or two days. Exhibitors rent spaces that are usually 8-foot by 8-foot or 10-foot by 10-foot, and the entry fee

Trial by Crafts

While plenty of shows are open to anyone who can pay the entry fee, the better shows are typically juried—that is, a panel of judges evaluates applications and chooses a limited number of exhibitors to be in the show.

You'll be asked to send photographs or slides of your work. This is not a place to cut corners. Your pictures must be as good as your work itself, because it's all the judges will see when they make their decision. Use good lighting and avoid cluttered backgrounds. Do something to show the work's scale—judges want to know if your work is 6 inches or 6 feet high.

If it's a show you've been in before, let the judges know you have something new to offer. "We don't send the same photos," Dianne Norman says of her woodworking business, Organize with Wood, that she runs with her husband, Jay, in De Land, Florida. "We send something that's very similar so they can identify us from the year before, but new items and a little note that says something like, 'We're working with more hardwoods this year,' or 'We have a new line of [whatever].' A lot of the shows want to change vendors every few years to make the show look new, so if you can change with them, you stand a better chance of getting in."

In addition to pictures, your application for a juried show should include your professional biography or resume, your artist's statement, a description of the processes and materials you use, a price list, brochures from other exhibitions, and copies of any newspaper or magazine articles about your work.

is generally modest. These events are often sponsored by community groups, schools, or churches as a way to raise money; because of that they often have a loyal following. They are usually promoted with notices listed in community newspapers and posted on bulletin boards.

Regional crafts shows often receive more exposure, and consequently are more expensive to enter. They usually have more stringent entry requirements. Many shows receive more applications than they can accommodate, so they screen exhibitors by requiring them to submit slides of their work, then make their selections based on those slides.

Some shows have adopted an application process that requires hopeful exhibitors to submit an application fee, a jury fee, jury slides, a resume, and a list of customers in the general area of the show. It's possible that you could spend from $10 to $150 to have your work considered, and still not be selected to exhibit at the show—although some of the more reputable shows will return your jury fee if you are not accepted. When you request an application to exhibit at a regional show, ask if the show is juried, what the selection process is, and what portion, if any, of the fees is refundable. As with community fairs, booths in regional shows range in size from 8-by-8 to 10-by-10, but cost anywhere from $150 to more than $500.

Once You're In

Once you've been accepted into a crafts show, find out what will be provided by asking the following questions:

- ○ What equipment does the show supply? Are tables, chairs, drapes, poles, lights, and electrical outlets provided? What is included in your basic fee, and what is extra?
- ○ What type of lighting is used? Some types of light will alter the color and general appearance of your crafts, which can decrease sales, particularly for jewelers and glass artists.
- ○ How much will electricity cost?
- ○ Does the facility use union or nonunion workers? If the facility uses union workers, you will have to pay more to have workers set up your tables and equipment.
- ○ Where do you load and unload your equipment and products?
- ○ How far away is parking? How much parking is available?
- ○ Are there hotels and restaurants nearby (if the show is not local)?
- ○ How many people attend the show?
- ○ How much advertising does the show promoter do?

Choosing a Show

The right show can generate substantial sales and profits; the wrong one can waste your valuable time and cost you money. But with literally thousands of arts and crafts shows, fairs and festivals held all over the country throughout the year, how do you choose the best ones for you? Do your homework. Talk to other craftspeople, study the show materials, and ask plenty of questions of the show's organizers or promoters.

Beware!
If a show promoter approaches you at a show, be wary. Professional promoters rarely approach crafters; they don't need to, because plenty of crafters seek them out based on the quality of their shows.

Some of the key things you'll need to know to make an informed decision about a show include:

- What is the foundation for the economy in the area where the show is held? Is it agricultural, manufacturing, or technology? Are attendees likely to be blue-collar or white-collar workers? This will give you an idea of the type of merchandise that will sell at the show and the price ranges people are likely to pay.

- What is the show's premise? Is it an arts and crafts show? Or is it a festival of some sort with crafts as an added attraction? If it's a festival, you may find most of the attendees more interested in the primary events than they are in shopping for crafts.

- How long has the show been held?

- If it's a repeat show, is it being run by the same people or an entirely new staff? Find out if anyone remembers how it was run last year and can tell you what's changed and why.

- How do the promoters define "handcrafted"? This could determine whether other exhibitors are true craftspeople or are sliding in with mass-produced items.

- What else, if anything, will be sold at the show besides art or crafts?

- How many exhibitors return each year? What percentage of this year's exhibitors are there for the first time? How many exhibitors are currently signed and how many are expected?

- How many exhibitors are in your product category?

- What is the expected show attendance? If it's a first-time show, ask what went into calculating that figure.

- How and where is the show being advertised? Does the promotion include spotlighting individual exhibitors?

Tip...

Smart Tip
If you're exhibiting alone, find out if the show provides professional booth-sitters who will keep an eye on your booth for short periods when you have to take a break.

It's also a good idea to ask the show's promoter candidly if he or she thinks your products are a good fit for the show, and why or why not.

Deb says choosing good shows has become even more challenging as the number of shows increases. "The market has become so saturated," she says, which makes the process of choosing shows more critical than ever.

Your Booth

Most crafters find that they must put the displays they use in their exhibits through several incarnations before they find the one that works best. Remember, your booth is the stage for your work; it needs to look great and function as a showroom and sales area. "You need to show off the most stock you can in the best possible way," says Dianne. "It's not as easy as it sounds."

"I made seven or eight different displays before finally arriving at the one we use now," says Jay. "We want the public to come into our area, to feel comfortable."

Dianne says she positions an unusual item at the front of the booth to attract people, which is a technique doll maker Gladys Johnson of Bunn, North Carolina, agrees with. The crafter behind Dolls by Gladys says, "You want something eye-catching so people will stop." You also need to be sure your display is spacious enough so that people can really see the items, and not just get the impression of clutter.

Use the design of your booth to help customers visualize how your items will look in their homes. By itself your booth doesn't need to be a work of art; instead, it needs to be a showcase for your work and a place that is comfortable and appealing to your customers.

Deb says she started out with tables, then had some bleachers built for her dolls. Now she uses crates that double as a display and carrying case. "We set the crates up in a staggered fashion, and we have baskets, dolls, and bunnies sitting all together like you would have on a shelf at home," she says. "We can carry all our merchandise and supplies to the show inside the crates."

Along with an attractive display, be sure you have a comfortable and efficient space to transact the actual sale. You need a place for your customers to put down their purses and bags when they're paying you or writing a check. You need room to process credit cards and make change for cash sales.

Keep transportation in mind. The best booth in the world is useless if you can't get it to a show. Make sure you can easily break it down to fit in your vehicle and still allow room for merchandise. Ideally, wall panels

Stat Fact

Research indicates that consumers make a decision about whether or not to stop at a booth in less than three seconds, and that decision is based on the visual elements of the booth.

Beware!

If your products are fragile, be sure your display protects them. Gladys Johnson of Bunn, North Carolina, makes sure her porcelain dolls are shielded from wind gusts that may knock them over, and that her nicer dolls are displayed high enough so they are out of the reach of children.

and framework should lay flat; you don't want to transport them upright or at an angle. To keep the weight down and make transporting easier, don't use solid walls; instead, create the illusion of a wall with stretched fabric.

When you're designing your booth, think about where your packing materials will go. Some shows offer out-of-booth storage areas, but you're better off if your boxes and other containers can fit into your booth components or be used for display.

Limit the walls of your booth to 8 feet high, which is the maximum for most shows. It's a good idea to design your booth to fit various-sized spaces because booth sizes can vary. Your basic booth could be 10-by-10 feet but designed in a way that allows it to be adjusted to 8-by-10 or 8-by-8 or even 6-by-8.

Keep as much merchandise as possible at eye level. Don't force customers to bend over or stretch up to see things. For most products, the ideal display height is 48 to 68 inches off the ground. Using varying levels will create visual interest and allow you to showcase individual pieces.

"A lot of times, midway through a show, I'll just move things around a little," Dianne says. "When people do their second trip back through the show, they may all of a sudden spot something they hadn't seen before, maybe because another customer was blocking it, or it wasn't at eye level or something."

Deb does the same thing. "When you change your display," she says, "it causes people—even people who know you and think they've seen everything you have—to stop because there is something different."

Consider lighting carefully. Depending on what your booth is made of, you may install track lighting on the walls or ceiling, or simply set up lamps that illuminate your merchandise. You may think you can't afford it, but a well-lit booth may quickly return the investment in strong sales. It doesn't do you any good to go to a show if people can't see your work.

Packing for a Crafts Show

Crafters are some of the friendliest people you'll ever meet, and most will be happy to lend you something you forgot to bring to a show, but it's best if you arrive with everything you need. Though your specific list will depend on your type of business, the following will help you develop your own customized crafts show supplies checklist:

- *Food and water.* You can never be sure about the availability and quality of drinking water; either bring your own, or bring jugs you can fill at a nearby fountain and take back to your booth. Concession-stand food is expensive and rarely the most healthy of fare, so bring snacks and your lunch. Choose items that are simple, can be consumed quickly and won't cause a mess.

Bright Idea

In addition to written directions to the show, be sure to write down the directions for getting home. That will be much easier to follow than trying to retrace your route when it's late and dark and you're exhausted.

- *Tools.* Wrench, hammer, pliers, nails, screwdriver, utility knife, tape measure.

- *Setting-up supplies.* Pins, tacks, and ties; wire; tape gun and tape; glue gun and glue; clamps and brackets; fishing line; tie-down ropes; weights; boards or wood blocks for leveling; sandpaper; dolly or handcart.

- *Display equipment.* All parts of your display, such as backdrops, signs, shelving, wall units, pegboards and hooks, risers, tables, chairs, stools, and other special displays.

- *Lighting.* Light fixtures, extra bulbs, extension cords, plug converter, power strip.

- *Coverings.* Table drapes, floor coverings, extra cloth, or curtain to be used for unexpected situations, plastic drop cloths or sheeting to protect your crafts from the elements or to cover them at night.

- *Demonstration items.* Whatever items are necessary to demonstrate your craft.

- *Promotional materials and sales aids.* Business cards, brochures, fliers, catalogs, artist's statement, portfolio, media kits, product samples.

- *Sale processing equipment.* Cash box or money apron, change for cash sales (adjust based on experience, but a good starting bank would include $50 in one-dollar bills, $30 in five-dollar bills, and $20 in coins), calculator, receipts, invoices, extra price tags, sales tax chart, mailing list sign-up sheet, credit card processing equipment and supplies, cellular phone, laptop computer.

- *Office supplies.* Pens, pencils, paper clips, stapler, rubber bands, scissors, paperweights, note paper, 3-by-5 cards, clipboard, tape.

- *Wrapping/packing supplies.* Bags, padding materials, tissue paper, tape, string.

- *Cleaning supplies.* Glass cleaner, paper towels, clean rags or cloths, feather duster, waste container, trash bags.

- *Personal items.* Clothing (in case of a spill or accident, and to allow for unexpected weather), extra shoes, ice chest, beverages, covered thermal drinking container, tissues and moist towelettes or baby wipes, sunscreen, skin lotion, first aid kit, sewing kit, safety pins, makeup, aspirin, antacids, a heater for winter shows, a fan for summer shows, emergency contact information.

- *Auto safety supplies.* Flashlight with fresh batteries, a can of flat tire repair product, spare tire and jack, maps, directions to the show.

- *Paperwork.* A copy of your show application and contract.

Booth Behavior

What you do and say while in your booth at a crafts show can have a tremendous impact on your success. Walk through a show, watch the exhibitors and think about whether you'd want to stop at their booths based on their behavior alone.

- *Don't just sit there.* When you're sitting there looking bored, you're telling potential customers that you're not excited about what you're doing, so why should they be? Or they may see you doing nothing, and fear that you're going to pounce on them desperately if they stop. So find something to do. Move around, rearrange your display, handle your administrative chores—whatever you do, keep busy.

- *Consider your place.* When Jay and Dianne first started doing shows, they sat outside the front of the booth and potential customers had to walk past them to see the merchandise. "That seemed to stop people from going in, because they wanted to look without talking, and they felt they had to talk to us to go past us," Dianne says. Sitting inside the booth didn't work, either, because they blocked their displays. "People don't want to walk up to you and look over your head," Jay says. They finally hit on the idea of a small opening at the back of the booth, where they can be visible but unobtrusive.

- *Demonstrate.* Do your craft while you're in the booth so people can see how you go from the raw materials to the finished product. Deb says it's a productive way to fill the down time while you're sitting in the booth, plus it attracts customers. "I sit there winding doll hair, trimming out dolls, stuffing dolls," she says. "Occasionally, my space will look like the Little Shop of Horrors because I've got arms, legs, and torsos, and it looks a little gruesome. But if you're working on your craft, you're not staring people down, wondering why they're not buying your stuff, and they will see that you're busy doing your thing, and they stop to watch you."

Bright Idea

You might be tempted to bring a book along to read during slow times at a show, but that's not the best idea. Look busy! Bring your laptop computer and do administrative work. Better yet, bring elements of your craft and do your craft—you'll be adding to your inventory and attracting attention at the same time.

- *Speak up.* Begin with a friendly greeting. Keep in mind that many people aren't sure what to say to an artist, so help them out by telling them something interesting about your craft. Make your comments brief, and give them a chance to respond and ask questions.

- *Smile.* Would you want to buy something from someone with a glum or scowling expression? Probably not. No matter how tired or frustrated you are, keep smiling—you never know which browser is going to turn into your next big sale, and besides, you'll feel better when you smile.

- *Take a break.* Periodically step away from your booth for a few minutes. Walk around the show, get some fresh air, have a snack or a drink.

> ### Smart Tip
> **Tip...**
>
> Be sure everything in your booth or store is clearly marked with the price. "Many people will not stop and ask you how much something costs," doll maker Deb Farish of Manchester, Missouri, says. "Don't let that be a reason a sale isn't made."

Craft Malls

If you decide to set up a booth at a craft mall, you would typically rent an 8-by-8 space, which could run anywhere from $50 to $125 a month. Larger booths are available at a higher price. Craft malls usually provide tables, but you need to supply your own table covering, decoration, displays, and, of course, your handcrafted goods.

Some craft malls allow you to exhibit your goods without your having to staff the booth. You can just rent the space, tag your goods, and leave everything else to the mall's employees. They will collect the money for the merchandise and sales tax, and provide security. These malls use tags they can run through a computerized cash register system, which keeps track of the items that were sold and how much was collected. Other malls require the exhibiting craftsperson to work at the mall several times each month.

Before renting a space in a craft mall, consider several issues. Does the craft mall have a sufficient customer base? Ask the mall operators for statistics and take the time to observe the traffic yourself. Do other retail shops surround the mall? Is it in an area that attracts a large number of shoppers, or would people have to travel specifically to the craft mall? Does the mall provide ample parking? Does the exhibit area have a security system? Does the mall take a percentage of your gross sales? Do you have to

> ### Bright Idea
> If you make clothing, be sure to keep a full-length mirror in your booth so customers can see how they'll look wearing your items.

work at the mall, and if so, for how many days each month? You might just have to staff your own booth, or you might have to operate the cash register or monitor inventory. Don't be afraid to ask questions. While craft malls suit the selling needs of many crafters, they don't suit them all.

Facility Design

If you have a homebased facility, your layout should have three separate areas: a work area, an inventory- and file-storage area, and an office area. You might have the same three areas if you have a studio located in a freestanding building. Some craftspeople, however, use their studio for production work but take care of administrative tasks in their homes. If you locate in a retail establishment, your floor space will be divided into a work area, an inventory storage area, an office area, and a display area. Again, you may choose to maintain an office area in your home, which would give you more selling space.

If you open your own retail store with your studio inside it, divide the store into thirds. You should put your bestsellers in the front third. This way, passersby will notice attractive items and enter your store. The middle portion of the store should hold your next bestsellers, and the least profitable items should be in the rear third.

Health and Safety

You may not give a great deal of thought to safety issues, particularly if you've been doing your craft as a hobby for years. But you need to. You face a wide range of physical risks that vary depending on your craft, such as working with sharp objects, temperature extremes, dangerous chemicals, or under other hazardous conditions. You have an obligation to yourself, your family, your employees, and even your customers to maintain a safe working environment.

Be sure all tools are used correctly and with the proper safety equipment, such as gloves, aprons, and eye protection. Chemicals should be used only according to the manufacturer's instructions, and stored and disposed of properly. Have an emergency first aid plan in place in case of an accident or injury.

Like many industrial and office workers, crafters are at risk of overuse injuries (also called cumulative trauma disorders, repetitive strain/stress injuries, and repetitive motion injuries), which can affect the upper and lower extremities and the back. A key risk factor in overuse injuries is performing the same movements over and over, such as using a computer keyboard and mouse, hand carving with a chisel, weaving, etc. Posture is another important issue; working in awkward positions or holding the same position for long periods of time can cause overuse injuries. You can also stress muscles and tendons if you exert excessive force while lifting, pulling, pushing, twisting, or gripping a tool or object.

The best way to deal with overuse injuries is prevention. Take an ergonomic approach by designing tools and equipment to the person and adapting the work process to the needs of the individual, not the other way around. Set up your work station in a way that allows you to use proper posture and minimizes musculoskeletal strain. Arrange tools and supplies within comfortable reach. Use proper tools for the job, and be sure they are in proper condition—for example, chisels, knives, scissors, etc. should be adequately sharpened with secure handles and grips.

> **Tip...**
>
> **Smart Tip**
>
> Don't allow smoking around any of your inventory items or packing materials. They will absorb the smell of cigarettes, and you may risk offending customers who are nonsmokers.

Security

Whether you work from home or a commercial location, keep security for yourself, your employees, and your property in mind. You likely have a considerable amount of equipment, finished products, and supplies that might be attractive to thieves or that could be destroyed in the event of a fire or natural disaster. These tips will help you avoid becoming a victim:

- Take a look at your home or commercial studio through the eyes of a criminal. How vulnerable are you? Your local police department may be able to assist you with a security analysis.

- Duplicate important data and store it off-site. Develop a system for regular backup procedures for your important business records and customer files to minimize your risk.

- Be sure all doors and windows close tightly and have effective locks.

- Check outside for potential access. Are there shrubs where a criminal could hide? If you work at home, do trees or a ladder near the house make it easy to access second-floor windows?

- Install exterior lighting using timers and/or motion sensors.

- When you're traveling, be sure someone will pick up mail, newspapers, and packages so your absence is not apparent to an observer.

- If other people, such as employees and service personnel, have keys to your house or studio, have the locks re-keyed once a year.

- If you work at home, think about how your business space relates to the living space in your house. Is it distinctly separate, and can it have its own locks and other security elements? Or is it integrated with the rest of your home and difficult to segregate?

- Consider an alarm system to protect both your personal and professional belongings. Today's alarm systems can do much more than simply notify police in the event of a break-in; they can monitor your home for fire, water damage, and even power failures. Systems can be zoned to offer different levels of protection in different sections of your house. Chimes can alert you to the opening of exterior doors and windows; this is particularly important if you work alone in a large house. Closed-circuit cameras allow you to see who is at your door before you open it; for even more advanced notice, a driveway annunciator can sound an interior chime when a vehicle pulls onto your property. Fixed or portable panic buttons can be programmed to notify police with or without an audible alarm.

Shop carefully for a security system. Though they are becoming increasingly affordable, price should be only a small part of your decision. Find out how long the company has been in business, if it has a local office, how its service is handled, how installers and technicians are trained, and if they are insured and bonded. Ask about the system's warranty, the cost of monitoring, and the length of contract. Get statistics on the company's history of apprehensions and scare-offs, and ask how many times the system has been beaten. Finally, ask for and check references.

Theft at Shows

Craft shows are not high crime events, but it is not unheard of for theft to occur at shows. Here are some tips to protect yourself against theft when you're exhibiting at a show:

- *Be aware that anyone may steal from you.* Thieves don't wear signs identifying their intent, so you need to accept the fact that anyone could be in your booth with the intent to steal. Don't be paranoid—after all, most people are trustworthy—but accept the reality that a few are not.

- *Stay alert.* When you're paying attention to what's going on around you, you're more attractive to prospective customers and much less attractive to thieves. They'll find an easier target who is less likely to remember them.

- *Theft-proof your booth.* Design your display with security in mind. Be sure you don't have loose corners or other openings at the sides or back that would allow someone to reach in and grab a piece of your work. Protect your cash box, money pouch, and purse by placing it in a sturdy box or other container that can't be easily snatched.

- *Be suspicious of distractions.* If someone is taking too much of your time or you just don't feel comfortable about something, take a moment to evaluate the situation. Criminals usually work in pairs, and it's not uncommon for one to be pretending to buy from you while another is stealing from you. Pay attention to everyone who is in your booth. If you suspect a potential shoplifter, let them know you're watching them and could identify them; one way is to comment on a physical characteristic, such as their hair or a tattoo.

- *Don't keep your cash in one place.* Separate it so that if you do get hit, you won't lose everything.
- *Keep checks and credit card slips separate from cash.*
- *Be discreet.* Don't make it obvious to a casual observer that you are carrying valuables (such as jewelry) or large sums of cash.
- *Be cautious about leaving valuables in hotel rooms.* If the hotel has in-room safes or a master safe, use them.
- *At the end of the show, pack up in a well-lighted area with lots of other people.* Never leave your keys in your vehicle while you're loading it. Once you're on the road, check to see if you're being followed by stopping in a public place a couple of times and looking around carefully. This might delay your trip home slightly, but it increases your chances of getting there with all your property and money.

Staffing Your
Business

Many crafts business owners, especially

those who operate part time, don't need any employees, and this

may be the case for you when you're first starting. In fact, many

successful crafts business owners often deliberately keep their

companies as one-person operations because they don't want to

deal with the headaches that growth brings. While there is

nothing wrong with this strategy, it does put a tremendous amount of pressure on you, and you may find yourself working 12 hours a day, six or seven days a week.

If your goal is growth, you will reach a point where you must hire people. If you open your own retail store, you will almost certainly need help. Or you might choose to work with sales reps to market your goods. Even if your goal isn't growth, there may be times when you need help, so it's important to understand the basics of finding, hiring, and managing personnel.

Some crafters enlist their family members for help. For example, a spouse might assist with record-keeping, and children might affix price tags on items, or even help make some items. Ideally, you should be paying these workers; if you can't afford to, at least come up with some way to compensate them for their efforts. And while there's nothing fundamentally wrong with using family members in your business, a too-casual approach can hamper your operation. Youngsters might not realize how important it is to complete a project on time, so you should set a schedule for them to follow. If they are not meeting deadlines, find out why. Are they not interested, or do they simply not have the ability to keep the pace you need? If they can't meet your demands, you have two options: complete the tasks yourself, or hire employees (non-family members) to take over the work.

Another circumstance when you might hire extra help is if the demand for your products is so great that you cannot fulfill the orders yourself. You might consider hiring part-timers to make products (or parts of them) on a piecework basis.

The first step in hiring is to decide exactly what you want someone to do. The job description doesn't have to be as formal as one you might expect from a large corporation, but it needs to clearly outline the person's duties and responsibilities. It should also list any special skills or other required credentials, such as a valid driver's license and clean driving record for someone who will be driving for you.

Next, you need to establish a pay scale. Salaries in the crafts industry are typically low, often not much more than minimum wage. But since employees tend to have an interest in crafts, they usually don't demand high wages.

> ## ⚠ Beware!
> Before you hire your first employee, make sure you are prepared. Have all your paperwork ready, know what you need to do in the way of tax reporting, and understand all the liabilities and responsibilities that come with having employees.

You should also have a job application form. You can get a basic form at most office supply stores, use the one provided in *Start-Up Basics*, or create your own. In any case, have your attorney review the form you'll be using for compliance with the most current employment laws.

Every prospective employee should fill out an application—even if it's someone you already know, and even if he or she has submitted a detailed resume. A resume is not a signed, sworn statement acknowledging that you can fire them if they lie, but the application is. The application will also help you verify their resumes; compare the two and make sure the information is consistent.

Now you're ready to start looking for candidates.

Recruiting

Don't limit employee applications to people who happen to call or stop in and ask for jobs—go out and recruit. Consider the requirements of the employees you are looking for: Do they need a talent for crafts? Do you have set hours, or can employees make their own hours as long as they complete the work on time? If you decide that homemakers or retired people would be suitable employees, consider where you may be able to recruit them. Contact nearby child-care centers and ask if any parents are looking for part-time work. Check with local senior citizens' centers to see if they have a job or information board. Ask for referrals from friends and professional colleagues. Ask everyone you come across—your sources of referrals are endless, and you never know who might know the perfect person for you.

Screening

Your time as the owner of a business is extremely valuable. When you post a job opening, you'll get plenty of responses from people who are not qualified. Save yourself time by screening applicants on the phone. Ask them if they have any experience working with crafts or in the particular type of work for which they are applying. Question them specifically about their qualifications. If they don't have the skills or experience, be direct; say something like "I'm looking for someone more experienced; I can't train an inexperienced person." This will reduce the number of people you have to interview face to face.

Interviewing and Evaluating

When you begin the hiring process, don't be surprised if you're as nervous at the prospect of interviewing potential employees as they are about being interviewed. After all, they may need a job—but the future of your company is at stake.

Stat Fact

Demographic projections indicate that finding good employees is going to be one of the biggest challenges all businesses face well into the 21st century.

It's a good idea to prepare your interview questions in advance. Develop open-ended questions that encourage the candidate to talk. In addition to knowing *what* they've done, you want to find out *how* they did it. Ask each candidate the same set of questions, and make notes as they respond so you can make an accurate assessment and comparison later.

If you're hiring people to make crafts, ask them to demonstrate their skills so you can see exactly what they do.

When the interview is over, let the candidate know what to expect. Is it going to take you several weeks to interview other candidates, check references, and make a decision? Will you want the top candidates to return for a second interview? Will you call the candidate, or should he or she call you? This is not only a good business practice, it's also common courtesy.

Always check former employers and personal references. Though many companies are very restrictive as to what information they'll verify, you may be surprised at what you can find out. Certainly you should at least confirm that the applicant told the truth about dates and positions held. Personal references are likely to give you some additional insight into the general character and personality of the candidate, and this will help you decide if they'll fit into your operation.

Be sure to document every step of the interview and reference-checking process. Even very small companies are finding themselves targets of employment discrimination suits. Good records are your best defense if it happens to you.

Once They're on Board

The hiring process is only the beginning of the challenge of having employees. The next thing you need to do is train them.

Many small businesses conduct their "training" by throwing someone into the job, but that's not fair to the employee, and it's certainly not good for your business. And if you think you can't afford to spend time on training, think again—can you afford *not* to adequately train your employees? Do you really want them making crafts or interacting with your customers when you haven't told them how you want things done?

In an ideal world, employees could be hired already knowing everything they need to know. But this isn't an ideal world, and if you want the job done right, you have to teach your people how to do it.

Whether done in a formal classroom setting or on the job, effective training begins with a clear goal, and a plan for reaching it. Training will fall into one of three major categories: orientation, which includes explaining company policies and procedures; job skills, which focuses on how to do specific tasks; and ongoing development, which enhances the basic job skills and grooms employees for future challenges and opportunities. These tips will help you maximize your training efforts:

> **Tip...**
>
> **Smart Tip**
>
> Training employees—even part-time, temporary help—to your way of doing things is extremely important. These people are representing you, and they need to know how to maintain the image and standards you've worked hard to establish.

- *Find out how people learn best.* Delivering training is not a one-size-fits-all proposition. People absorb and process information differently, and your training method needs to be compatible with their individual preferences. Some people like to read a manual, others prefer a spoken explanation, and still others need to see a demonstration. In a group-training situation, your best strategy is to use a combination of methods. When you're working one on one, tailor your delivery to fit the needs of the person you're training.

  With some employees, figuring out how they learn best can be a simple matter of asking them. Others may not be able to tell you because they don't understand it themselves; in those cases, experiment with various training styles and see what works best for the specific employee.

- *Use simulation and role-playing to train, practice, and reinforce.* One of the most effective training techniques is simulation, which involves showing an employee how to do something, then allowing him or her to practice it in a safe, controlled environment. If the task includes interpersonal skills, let the employee role-play with you or a co-worker to practice what he or she should say and do in various situations.

- *Be a strong role model.* Don't expect more from your employees than you are willing to do. You're a good role model when you do things the way they should be done all the time. Don't take shortcuts you don't want your employees to take or behave in any way you don't want them to behave. On the other hand, don't assume that simply doing things the right way is enough to teach others how to do things. Role modeling is not a substitute for training; it reinforces training. If you role model but never train, employees aren't likely to get the message.

- *Look for training opportunities.* Once you get beyond basic orientation and job skills training, you need to be constantly on the lookout for opportunities to enhance the skill and performance level of your people.

- *Make it real.* Whenever possible, use real-life situations to train—but avoid letting customers know they've become a training experience for employees.

- *Anticipate questions.* Don't assume that employees know what to ask. In a new situation, people often don't understand enough to formulate questions. Anticipate their questions and answer them in advance.

- *Ask for feedback.* Finally, encourage employees to let you know how you're doing as a trainer. Just as you evaluate their performance, convince them that it's OK to tell you the truth. Ask them what they thought of the training and your techniques, and use that information to improve your own skills.

Employee Benefits

The actual wages you pay may be only part of your employees' total compensation. While many very small companies do not offer a formal benefits program, more and more business owners have recognized that benefits—particularly in the area of insurance—are extremely important when it comes to attracting and retaining quality employees. Regardless of whether the employment rate is up or down, competition for good people is stiff. Typical benefit packages include group insurance (your employees may pay all or a portion of their premiums), paid holidays, and vacations. You can build employee loyalty by seeking additional benefits that may be somewhat unusual—and they don't have to cost much. For example, if you're in a retail location, talk to other store owners in your shopping center to see if they're interested in providing reciprocal employee discounts. You'll not only provide your own employees with a benefit, but you may get some new customers out of the arrangement.

For more on employee benefits, policies, and procedures, and other human resources issues, see Chapter 6 in *Start-Up Basics*.

If the Unthinkable Happens

In most states, if you have three or more employees, you are required by law to carry workers' compensation insurance. This coverage pays medical expenses and replaces a portion of the employee's wages if he or she is injured on the job. Even if you have only one or two employees, you may want to consider this coverage to protect both them and you in the event of an accident.

Details and requirements vary by state; contact your state's insurance office or your own insurance agent for information so you can be sure you are in compliance. You'll also find more information in Chapter 6 in *Start-Up Basics*.

Equipping Your
Business

The equipment you'll need to run your crafts business falls into two basic categories: the tools and supplies you need specifically to make your handcrafted items, and the equipment you need to operate your business such as your office and display equipment.

Craft-Making Equipment

If you've been doing your craft as a hobby, you probably already have the basic necessary items. As you make the transition from hobbyist to professional, you may decide to add equipment to enhance your production. The following section will take a look at the basic equipment required for some of the more popular types of crafts and what you can expect to spend.

- *Ceramics.* The basic materials ceramists need are clay, glaze, and paint, which are all very inexpensive when they're purchased in bulk. You'll need a potter's wheel for shaping the items and a kiln for baking them. Wheels start at about $250 for one with no motor, and go up to about $800. Typically, kilns range from $500 to $1,800, depending on size, but they can go as high as $13,000. You'll also need tools for trimming and carving the clay and brushes for painting the items. You can probably get started with as little as $50 worth of tools, but you could easily spend considerably more on items you will use.

- *Floral crafts.* The basic supplies you need for floral crafts are artificial and dried flowers. You'll also need a stock of artificial leaves, moss, and ribbon. Flowers cost from less than $1 to $10 per item, depending on the materials used and the quality of the item. You'll also need wire cutters, a glue gun, glue, and green wire. Expect to spend about $50 on these items.

- *Jewelry.* The type of supplies you'll need depends on whether you're making expensive or inexpensive jewelry. For higher-priced items, you'll need gold, silver, and gemstones. You can make lower-priced products out of anything from plastic to beads. You'll need cutting tools, pliers, and files, and for some items, you may want paint. Expect to spend anywhere from $50 to more than $300 on these tools. You might also need a soldering iron (typically $40 to $100), a microscope for inspecting gemstones (typically several hundred dollars, but high-end models can cost up to $5,000), and a workbench (about $100).

- *Sewing.* Needed materials vary depending on what you're making, but likely will include fabric, batting, seam binding, interfacing, Velcro, elastic, buttons, lace, hooks and eyes, lining, and thread. These are reasonably priced items, and how much you spend depends on the quantity you buy. You'll also need a sewing machine ($200 to $400, or higher), an iron and ironing board (about $30 to $40), and a cutting board ($30 to $50). Other supplies

Dollar Stretcher

Many supplies will send samples of their products, usually at no charge, so be sure to check out their products before you buy. Candle maker Melony Bell says the fragrance oil companies she buys from will send up to 20 samples at a time for free.

include needles, pins, scissors, pinking shears, marking chalk, a tape measure, and a thimble. Most of these items cost only a few dollars each, although quality scissors and pinking shears run $20 or more.

Bright Idea
Whatever craft you do, if you need to measure things, this will help: To make writing down dimensions easier, glue a pad of small self-stick notes to the side of your tape measure; you'll always have paper when you need it to record a measurement.

- *Needlecraft.* To do most needlecraft projects, you'll need embroidery floss, yarn, Aida cloth, fabric, ribbons, and frames for wall hangings. You will also need scissors and needles. You probably won't spend more than $5 for the fabric, yarn, and embroidery floss for any given project. A supply of needles will cost just a few dollars, and you should expect to spend $20 or so on a good pair of scissors.

- *Crocheting and knitting.* In addition to the required yarn and ribbon, which will generally cost only a few dollars per item, you'll need knitting needles, a crochet hook, and scissors. The needles and hook should cost about $2 to $5, and the scissors about $20.

- *Woodworking.* Wood costs will vary depending on the type of wood you choose to work with, its availability, and the quality and quantity you need. Woodworker Jay Norman of DeLand, Florida, says he gets most of his wood from building supply stores. He shops around and gets to know people so they understand his needs. You'll also need more equipment than many other crafters, including a

Broke-In or Broken?

Should you buy all new equipment, or will used be sufficient? That depends, of course, on which equipment you're thinking about.

For office furniture (desks, chairs, filing cabinets, bookshelves, etc.), you can get some great deals buying used items. You might also be able to save a significant amount of money buying certain office equipment—such as your copier, phone system, and fax machine—used rather than new. However, for high-tech items, such as your computer, you'll probably be better off buying new. Don't try to run your company on outdated technology.

To find good used equipment, you'll need to shop around. Certainly check out used office furniture and equipment dealers. Also check the classified section of your local paper under items for sale, as well as notices of bankrupt companies and companies that are going out of business and need to liquidate.

table saw ($270 to $800), a band saw ($150 to $300), a sander (hand-held models range from $30 to $200), a drill press ($100 to $600 or more), a plane ($10 to $30), squares ($5 to $20), and files (average $10 each).

- *Wood-carving.* The basic materials wood-carvers use are wood, paint, and glaze. Wood can be bought in the form of boards, blanks, and roughouts. Blanks are blocks of wood that need to be carved and detailed. Roughouts are already roughly carved in a specific shape, but they need detailing. Tools include rotary carving tools, chisels, knives, and gouges. A beginning wood-carver can buy a knife and a set of gouges for about $50. Chisel prices range from $20 to $60, while electric chisels cost from $175 to more than $400. A rotary carving tool sells for about $150. To protect yourself from cuts, you should wear a sturdy glove on the hand with which you hold the wood; expect to pay $20 to $25 for this safety item.

- *Glass.* The materials needed to work in glass include dye (paint), glass, and lead. Equipment includes a soldering iron ($40 to $100), glass cutters ($4 to $11), and a kiln for glass sculptures (ranging from a few hundred dollars to more than $3,000, depending on size).

Whatever your equipment, it will likely need regular maintenance: knives need to be sharpened, saws oiled, sewing machines cleaned. Use the form on page 73 to help you keep a regular maintenance schedule.

Basic Office Equipment

Management and administration are critical parts of any business, and you need the right tools to handle these tasks. Your office equipment needs will vary significantly depending on the size of your operation. (See the chart on page 74 for the equipment and supplies needed for two hypothetical crafts businesses). Use the information in this chapter as a guideline, but make your final decisions based on your situation.

As tempting as it may be to fill up your office with an abundance of clever gadgets designed to make your working life easier and more fun, you're better off disciplining yourself to buy only the bare necessities. Consider these basic items:

- *Typewriter.* You may think that most typewriters are in museums these days, but they remain quite useful to businesses that deal frequently with preprinted and multipart forms, such as contracts, government forms, and show applications. A good electric typewriter can be purchased for $100 to $200.

- *Computer and printer.* A computer is an essential piece of equipment for any business. It will help you handle the financial side of your business and produce marketing materials. You don't necessarily need the "latest and greatest" in computer power, but PC users need a system that uses Windows, a Pentium processor, 32 to 48MB RAM, a minimum 3GB hard drive, CD-ROM or DVD-ROM, and a 56K modem. Mac users should find that the basic iMac covers their needs. Expect to spend $1,500 to $3,500 for your computer, and an additional $200 to $1,000 for a printer.

- *Software.* Think of software as your computer's brains, the instructions that tell your computer how to accomplish the functions you need. There are many programs on the market that will handle your accounting, customer information management, and other administrative requirements. You'll also want to take a look at the programs designed specifically for crafters. Software can be a significant investment, so do a careful analysis of your needs, then study the market and examine a variety of products before making a final decision.

- *Modem.* Modems are necessary to access online services and the Internet; they have become a standard component of most computers. If you are going to

Equipment Maintenance Form

Whether your equipment consists of sewing supplies, power tools, kilns, or something else, all equipment needs regular maintenance to function properly and safely. Temperature, humidity, usage, ventilation, and friction can cause wear on equipment. See the manufacturer's guidelines for information on necessary internal and external maintenance, set up schedules and keep logs to document the work you've done. This will also help if you ever have a warranty claim on a piece of equipment and the manufacturer challenges it.

Date _____

Equipment _____

_____

Work performed:

❑ Adjusted ❑ Patched ❑ Lubricated

❑ Cleaned ❑ Repaired ❑ Replaced part #_____

Notes:

_____

_____

Equipment and Supplies Costs

This equipment table represents the equipment required by two hypothetical crafts businesses with annual sales of $13,000 and $190,000 respectively. The low-end example represents a part-time crafter who makes stuffed animals and children's clothing. She exhibits at crafts shows three times a month during the summer and early fall and has been in business for three years. The high-end example represents a full-time ceramist who has owned his own business for 15 years and sells his items through wholesale crafts shows and mail order.

The part-time crafter has no employees and works from a 200-square-foot homebased office. The ceramist rents a 750-square-foot studio in an industrial area and employs one full-time worker who assists in making pottery and handles light clerical work.

Because each craftsperson in this example makes different kinds of crafts, they require different kinds of equipment, which is reflected in the equipment costs.

Item	Low	High
Specialty Equipment		
Glue gun	$10	$0
Carving tools	0	20
Sewing machine	300	0
Scissors	20	0
Paint brushes	10	50
Potter's wheel	0	650
Kiln	0	2,500
Bench	0	250
Signage	0	400
Security system	0	1,500
Office Furniture/Equipment		
Computer	1,200	5,000
Chair(s)	100	175
Desk(s)	400	750
File cabinets	60	150
Calculator/tape	80	160

Equipment and Supplies Costs, continued

Answering machine	60	145
Copier	0	1,200
Fax machine	0	350
Miscellaneous desktop items (calendars, document baskets, etc.)	30	100
Lighting	70	150
Phone	33	150
Packaging/Shipping Equipment		
Hand truck	0	125
High-speed tape dispensers	0	25
Carton stapler	0	500
UPS/Parcel post scale	0	400
Total Costs	**$2,373**	**$14,750**

conduct any business online, whether it's networking with other crafters, creating your own Web site to attract customers, doing research or simply communicating via e-mail, you must have a modem. For more about purchasing a computer, printer, software, and peripherals, see Chapter 8 of *Start-Up Basics*.

- *Photocopier.* The photocopier is a fixture of the modern office, but not a necessity for most small craft operations. However, if you decide you need one, you can get a basic, low-end, no-frills personal copier for less than $400 in just about any office supply store. More elaborate models increase proportionately in price. If you anticipate a heavy volume of photocopying, consider leasing.

- *Fax machine.* Fax capability has become another must in modern offices, and are necessary for crafters if you want to take orders via fax. You can either add a fax card to your computer or buy a stand-alone machine. If you use your computer, it must be turned on to send or receive faxes, and the transmission may interrupt other work. For most businesses, a stand-alone machine on a dedicated telephone line is a wise investment. A fax machine can also double as a low-volume copier. Expect to pay $150 to $300 for a fax machine.

- *Postage scale.* Unless all your mail is identical, a postage scale is a valuable investment. An accurate scale takes the guesswork out of postage and will quickly pay for itself. It's a good idea to weigh every piece of mail to eliminate

▲

the risk of items being returned for insufficient postage or overpaying when you're unsure of the weight. Light mailers—1 to 12 articles per day—will be adequately served by inexpensive mechanical postal scales, which typically range from $10 to $25. If you're averaging 12 to 24 items per day, consider a digital scale, which is somewhat more expensive—generally from $50 to $200—but significantly more accurate than a mechanical unit. If you send more than 24 items per day or use priority or expedited services frequently, invest in an electronic computing scale, which weighs the item and then calculates the rate via the carrier of your choice, making it easy for you to make comparisons. Programmable electronic scales range from $80 to $250.

- *Postage meter.* Postage meters allow you to pay for postage in advance and print the exact amount on the mailing piece. Many postage meters can print in increments of one-tenth of a cent, which can add up to big savings for bulk mail users. Meters also provide a professional image, are more convenient than stamps, and can save you money in a number of ways. Postage meters are leased, not sold, with rates starting at about $30 per month. They require a license, which is available from your local post office. Only four manufacturers are licensed by the U.S. Postal Service to manufacture and lease postage meters; your local post office can provide you with contact information. Most crafters can get by comfortably using stamps rather than a postage meter for regular mail. But if you are shipping products through the USPS, a meter and good scales may be a worthwhile investment.

- *Paper shredder.* A response to both a growing concern for privacy and the need to recycle and conserve space in landfills, shredders are becoming increasingly common in both homes and offices. They allow you to efficiently destroy incoming unsolicited direct mail, as well as sensitive internal documents before they are discarded. Light-duty shredders start at about $25, and heavier-capacity shredders run $150 to $500.

See the chart on page 79 for minor—but still necessary—office supplies.

Telecommunications

The ability to communicate quickly with your customers, employees, and suppliers is essential to any business. Advancing technology gives you a wide range of telecommunications options. Most telephone companies have created departments dedicated to small and homebased businesses. Contact your local service provider and ask to speak with someone who can review your needs and help you put together a service and equipment package that will work for you. Specific elements to keep in mind include:

- *Telephone.* Whether you're homebased or in a commercial location, you should install two phone lines—one for voice, another for fax and/or modem. As you grow and your call volume increases, you may need to add more lines.

Your telephone can be a tremendous productivity tool, and most of the models on the market today are rich in features you will find useful. Such features include automatic

> **Bright Idea**
> Periodically call your voice mail to see how it sounds. Make sure what your customers hear is clear and professional.

redial, which redials the last number called at regular intervals until the call is completed; programmable memory for storing frequently called numbers; and a speaker phone for hands-free use. You may also want call forwarding, which allows you to forward calls to another number when you're not at your desk, and call waiting, which signals you that another call is coming in while you are on the phone. Caller ID let's you know who is calling. These services are typically available through your telephone company for a monthly fee.

If you're going to be spending a great deal of time on the phone, perhaps doing marketing or handling customer service, consider a headset for comfort and efficiency. A cordless phone lets you take the phone with you as you move around your workspace. These units vary widely in price and quality, so research them thoroughly before making a purchase.

- *Answering machine/voice mail.* Because your business phone should never go unanswered, you need some sort of reliable answering device to take calls when you can't do it yourself. Whether you buy an answering machine (expect to pay $40 to $150 for one that is suitable for a business) or use the voice-mail service provided through your telephone company depends on your personal preferences, work style, and needs.

- *Cellular phone.* Once considered a luxury, cellular phones have become standard equipment for most business owners. Most have features similar to your office phone, such as caller ID, call waiting, and voice mail. Equipment and service packages are very reasonably priced. For crafters who exhibit at shows and fairs, cellular phones are especially important, particularly at outdoor events, because they allow you to immediately access credit card information and checking accounts to verify funds. They also provide additional security when you're on the road.

- *Pager.* A pager lets you know that someone is trying to reach you and lets you decide when to return the call. Many people use pagers in conjunction with cellular phones to conserve the cost of air time. Ask prospective pager suppliers if your system can be set up so you are paged whenever someone leaves a message in your voice-mail box. This service allows you to retrieve your messages immediately and eliminates having to check periodically to see if anyone has called. As with cellular phones, the pager industry is very competitive, so shop around for the best deal.

▲

- *E-mail.* E-mail is rapidly becoming a standard element in a company's communication package. It allows for fast, efficient, trackable 24-hour communication. Check your messages regularly and reply to them promptly.

Other Equipment

Some of the other miscellaneous equipment you'll need to consider include:

- *Cash register.* Whether you're selling in a retail store, at shows and fairs, or other retail outlets, you need a way to track sales, collect money, and make change. You can do this with something as simple as a divided cash drawer and a printing calculator, or you can purchase a sophisticated, state-of-the-art, point-of-sale system, which is networked with your computer. Of course, the latter will cost somewhere between $1,200 and $5,000 per terminal, and may not be a practical investment for a small crafts operation. Another option is an electronic cash register (ECR), which can range from $600 to $3,000, and can be purchased outright, leased, or acquired under a lease-purchase agreement. The newer ECRs offer such options as payment records to designate whether a customer paid by cash, check, or charge; department price groupings (appropriate for retail stores with multiple departments—not a feature you're likely to use); sign-in keys to help you monitor cashiers and clerks; and product price groups (which lets you organize products as they are rung up) for tracking inventory more effectively.

- *Credit and debit card processing equipment.* This could range from a simple imprint machine to an online terminal. Consult with several merchant account providers to determine the most appropriate and cost-effective equipment for your operation.

- *Security.* Whether you are homebased, have a commercial studio, or rent space in a retail outlet, consider a security system to protect your equipment and inventory.

Office Supplies

You'll likely require very little in the way of office supplies—but what you need to keep on hand is important.

Be sure to maintain an adequate stock of marketing materials including brochures, business cards, etc. You'll also need to maintain an ample supply of administrative items including checks, invoices, receipts, stationery, paper, and miscellaneous office supplies. Local stationers and office supply stores will have most or all the miscellaneous office supplies you need.

Inventory

The size of your finished product inventory depends on what you make and where you exhibit. In the beginning, your inventory can be relatively small, especially if you're just selling to friends and relatives on a one-to-one basis. In fact, it's best to avoid building a large inventory at this stage because you may end up getting stuck with items that aren't selling. Start small and see what moves.

Some crafters operate in a way that allows them to keep a minimal inventory. For example, Lynn Korff of Korff's Ceramic Originals in Cabot, Pennsylvania, paints her ceramics to order, so she doesn't keep a finished product inventory. She keeps a minimal amount of ready-to-paint stock on hand, and for

Beware!

When you're buying in bulk, be careful not to overbuy on trendy items or colors that may become outdated quickly; you may be unable to sell the products you make with those materials. Bulk purchases are best for staple-type items that can be used year in, year out.

Office Supplies Checklist

In addition to office equipment, you'll need an assortment of minor office supplies. Those items include:

❑ Scratch pads

❑ Staplers, staples, and staple removers

❑ Tape and dispensers

❑ Scissors

❑ "Sticky" notes in an assortment of sizes

❑ Paper clips

❑ Plain paper for your printer and copier if you have one

❑ Paper and other supplies for your fax machine (if you have one)

❑ Letter openers

❑ Pens, pencils, and holders

❑ Correction fluid (to correct typewritten or handwritten documents)

❑ Trash cans

❑ Desktop document trays

▲

most of her supplies, she says, "I pretty much just get it as I need it. I try not to have a lot of inventory because I don't have a lot of room to store things."

When you are exhibiting at larger retail crafts shows, you'll need to carry a more extensive inventory. Some crafts shows require that all vendors bring enough of their

---

Wrapping Up the Scale

If you're going to be selling retail, either in a store or at crafts fairs, you'll need certain supplies depending on your particular craft. Use this list as a guide:

○ Pricing guns and labels

○ Tagging guns and supplies

○ Merchandise bags—can be plain plastic bags, paper shopping bags with handles, or gift bags

○ Jewelry displays, velvet or economy

○ Earring displays and mirrors

○ Jewelry pouches, folders, rolls, cases, trays

○ Jewelry boxes—ring, earring, necklace boxes—either plain or specially designed

○ Gift boxes, bows, and ribbons

○ Stationery boxes

○ Tissue paper

○ Shredded grass

○ Cello film

○ Polybags

○ Heat sealers

○ Garment bags

○ Twist ties

○ Trash can liners

○ Shrink systems, wrap, and bags

○ Sign cards

○ Glue guns and glue sticks

You'll also need display fixtures, such as storage shelves and cabinets, partitions or paneling, fold-out tables, lights, and a checkout counter.

---

goods to last for the duration of the show. If you sold all of your goods on Friday at a show that runs through Sunday, you would be cheating yourself and the attendees, and the show organizers wouldn't be happy about having an empty booth. Certainly selling all your items in one day sounds great, but if you could have sold more on the following days, that would mean you lost money because you didn't generate the income you could have, and you would still have to pay the entire show fee.

> ### Smart Tip
> Tip...
>
> Keeping unsold inventory on hand is expensive and a waste of space. If something hasn't sold in reasonable time, get rid of it. Either mark it down and absorb the loss as a business lesson, or donate it to charity and take the tax deduction.

Candle maker Melony Bell of Fort Meade, Florida, says maintaining inventory when you're selling to retail stores is much easier than when you're selling at crafts shows. "Stores will give me two or three months' notice of what they want," she says. "But the crafts shows—you never know what you're going to sell. What worked at one show won't always work at the next."

Ordering supplies on a timely basis is an important part of maintaining inventory. If you wait too long to order supplies, your basic stock of finished products could run low and you'll lose sales and customers. On the other hand, you don't want to tie up too much of your financial resources in maintaining a stock of supplies you aren't using.

Tracking Inventory

A critical part of managing inventory is tracking it—that means knowing what you have on hand, what's on order, and when it will arrive, and what you have sold. This information allows you to plan your purchases intelligently, quickly recognize fast-moving items that need to be restocked, and identify slow-moving merchandise that you might want to consider marking down to move out.

You have a variety of inventory-tracking methods to choose from, from basic hand-written records to computerized barcode systems. The crafts business owners we talked to use simple systems, most by hand and some on basic computer databases. You could, for example, just add items to an inventory list as you make them, then check them off as you sell them. The larger you want your business to grow, the more sophisticated your inventory management will need to be. Your accountant or computer consultant can help you develop a system that will work for your particular situation.

> ### Bright Idea
> If your storage space is limited, try negotiating a deal like this with your suppliers: Make a long-term purchase commitment to earn volume pricing, but arrange for delivery in increments so you don't have to store the materials.

Buying Resources

Bright Idea

Ask other crafters who they buy from. Most are happy to share their supplies and recommendations (and warnings!) with fellow craftspeople.

Depending on your particular needs, you may need a few suppliers or dozens or even none at all. Part-time craftspeople typically don't make their products in large enough quantities to contract with wholesale suppliers; a visit to the local fabric or crafts store will meet their needs. If you have unusual materials needs, or if your business grows to the point where you can place large orders directly with suppliers to reduce your costs, you might need to look beyond local sources. Some suppliers will contact you through their sales reps. More often, particularly when you're starting out, you'll need to locate suppliers at trade shows, through buyers' directories, industry contacts, and trade journals.

A crafts business is only as good as its wares. Reliable suppliers, retailers, and sales reps will steer you toward hot-selling items that can increase your sales. However, it's your money and you should analyze any advice, use common sense and be aware of what your customers want. Suppliers can be divided into two general categories:

1. *Manufacturers.* Most craftspeople buy through company salespeople or independent representatives who handle the wares of several different companies. Prices are usually lowest from these sources unless your location makes the freight costly.

2. *Distributors.* Also known as wholesalers, brokers, or jobbers, these operators use quantity discounts to buy from two or more manufacturers and then warehouse the goods for sale to crafters. Although their prices are higher than a manufacturer's, they can supply you with small orders from a variety of sources. (Some manufacturers refuse to break case lots to fill small orders.) Also, the lower freight bill and quick delivery time from a nearby distributor will often compensate for the higher per-item cost.

You might also purchase supplies at trade shows where major suppliers display their products. Practically every major city hosts one or

Smart Tip

Don't always trust that your suppliers have sent the correct product; check it before you use it. Melony Bell of Fort Meade, Florida, once made the mistake of making 800 candles with the wrong grade of wax. Though the supplier replaced the wax, she still had to deal with replacing the candles she sold and soothing unhappy customers.

more trade shows relevant to crafts. Your local chamber of commerce or convention bureau can give you information on upcoming shows. Crafts trade shows are also listed in a number of magazines; see the Appendix for a list of publications.

Vehicle

One of the most important pieces of equipment for a craftsperson is your vehicle, whether it's a car, van, or truck. You will need to transport your crafts items to shows and stores, as well as visit suppliers and retailers, and attend business and professional association meetings. You can use your own vehicle if it is suitable, or lease or purchase one that will better meet your needs. Either way, keep good records of your automobile expenses, because they are tax deductible.

Jay and his wife, Dianne, have a pickup truck with a topper that they use for their company, Organize with Wood. "I have two roof racks, so our display and canopy goes on the roof," Jay says. "The truck has a big backseat, which I take out when we go to shows." He packs that area efficiently, being careful not to block his rearview vision with boxes.

Candlemaker Melony Bell bought a trailer to hitch to her car. She found that leaving her display and other show equipment in the trailer was more convenient than loading a truck or van for shows.

Marketing Your
Business

Most crafters begin their businesses through word-of-mouth advertising. You give or sell one of your crafts to someone; that person's friends, family members, or co-workers see the item and those who like it ask how they can obtain one; your name is mentioned, and you have an order for another item. As demand for your products grows, you start to look for ways to sell more of them. And now you need to use traditional means of business promotion to inform current and potential customers of what you have to offer and how they can find you.

Marketing is something many people don't like to do, but it can be as creative and as much fun as making your crafts. And no matter how clever and attractive your crafts are, they won't sell themselves—you need to market them. Use your imagination and always be receptive to new ideas and techniques.

To develop a marketing plan, you need to be very clear on what you are selling, the image you want to project, and the market you are trying to reach.

Defining Your Product and Image

Defining your product is fairly simple: It's a description of what you make. Articulating your image so you know what to emphasize in your marketing materials takes a little work. Answer these questions:

- *What products are you offering?* What is special about them beyond their obvious appearance and function? For example, do they use recycled materials or are they in some other way environmentally friendly?

- *What is the quality of the products you sell?* For example, will the wind chimes you make survive the elements? Are the baskets sturdy enough to use, or are they simply decorative?

- *What kind of image do you want to project?* Are you selling inexpensive, impulse-type items? Or do you want to make collector's pieces? Are your products original and unique, or do other crafters make the same things?

- *How do you compare with the competition?* Are your prices competitive? Are your products of lesser, comparable or greater quality?

Targeting Your Market

In Chapter 3, you learned how to identify your market. As you put together your marketing strategy, you need to further define your market, your goals, and your relationship to your customers. To do that, you should be able to answer these questions:

- *Who are your potential customers?* If you make baby blankets and clothes, your market would most likely consist of parents and relatives of newborn babies. If you make home decor items, your market will be adult women in an income range that allows them to afford your products.

- *How many are there?* Knowing how many potential customers you have will help you determine if you can build a sustainable business.

- *Where are they?* Is there a substantial market in your local area? Will people around the country buy your items?

- *Where do they now purchase the crafts you plan to sell?* For example, are they buying baby items from department stores or specialty shops?

- *What can you offer that they're not getting now, and how can you persuade them to do business with you?* In other words, what would be their motivation to buy from you instead of their current sources? Are you offering a better value? Greater quality? Can you personalize items?

You've probably already answered most of these questions when you did your market research. Now it's time to expand that information and use it to construct a marketing program.

> **Bright Idea**
> When a customer pays with a personal check, use the information (name and address) from the check to build your mailing list.

Advertising

Craftspeople usually don't spend very much on advertising, but there are times when it's a worthwhile investment. When you exhibit at shows, the sponsor will usually handle advertising and promotion, although you may want to supplement that effort with a small direct-mail campaign.

The advertising media generally used by craftspeople are:
- Word-of-mouth
- Magazines
- Newspapers
- Newsletters
- Telephone directories
- Direct mail
- Catalogs, handouts, brochures

Choosing the advertising medium is particularly challenging for small operations like a part-time crafts business. Typically, big-city television, radio, and newspapers are too expensive. Magazines are expensive and cover too broad an area to be cost-effective (unless you are selling by mail order). You may find small local newspapers and community publications to be reasonably priced; you'll know whether they will be effective for you only if you try them.

> **Smart Tip** *Tip...*
> Word-of-mouth is the most important form of advertising for a craftsperson. Each happy customer can steer dozens of new ones to you. Make sure that business cards and/or fliers are always available for customers to pass on to others, and include them in the package with each sale.

When you're evaluating prospective advertising media, consider these factors:

- *Cost per contact.* How much will it cost to reach each prospective customer?
- *Frequency.* How frequent should the contacts be? Is a single powerful advertisement preferable to a series of constant small reminders, or vice versa?

> ### Bright Idea
> When you're exhibiting in a crafts show, send a postcard to existing customers in the area where the show will take place to let them know you'll be there.

- *Impact.* Does the medium appeal to the appropriate senses, such as sight and hearing, in presenting design, color, or sound?
- *Selectivity.* To what degree can the message be restricted to those people who are known to be the most logical prospects?

Think through your advertising/marketing decisions carefully, and don't feel pressured to do things unless you're reasonably sure based on your own assessment—not just the assurances of the ad salesperson—that they will work. For example, giving your crafts to a charity will likely benefit you only if you have a retail site that can be promoted through the event or if there's going to be a show in the area immediately following the give-away. If your market is adults, don't advertise in publications that are directed to teenagers. And no matter who your market is, don't buy the expensive four-color brochure when a two-color flier will do. See Chapter 10 in *Start-Up Basics* for more on marketing and advertising.

Consignment Sales

Consignment sales, mentioned in Chapter 6, can be an excellent way to market and sell your work. In a consignment arrangement, you, as the owner of the merchandise, deliver or consign those goods to a consignee, typically a retail store. The consignee attempts to sell the goods, and upon doing so, earns a commission, which is deducted from the proceeds paid to you, the consignor.

You retain ownership of the merchandise until it is sold, so you need to be sure your property is protected. Always obtain a receipt for any items placed for consignment sale. The receipt should describe the item(s) consigned, the agreed-on sales price, the commission, the length of the consignment, and payment arrangements. Your agreement should also address who is responsible for loss or damage to the merchandise, as well as how it will be displayed.

Check out any shop that you deal with on a consignment basis carefully. Be sure it's an established concern; you don't want to leave your goods and return a month later to find the shop closed and the owner nowhere to be found. The shop should be easily accessible, neat, and attractive with friendly, helpful salespeople. It should carry other items similar or related to yours.

Consignment fees vary, but 50 percent is not unreasonable. Be sure you have structured your prices so that you can pay the consignment fee and still make a profit on your work.

It's a good idea to drop in regularly to check on your work. Be sure it is displayed to its best advantage. If your inventory is low, talk to the shop owner about restocking; if certain items aren't moving, consider taking them back and replacing them with something else.

Many states have passed consignment laws that protect craftspeople. Before placing items for consignment, find out what the laws are in your state by checking with your attorney or contacting your Department of Commerce for assistance.

Using Sales Representatives

If you don't have the time or inclination to do your own selling, consider hiring people to do it for you. There are professional manufacturers' sales representatives who make their living selling lines of goods to retailers; however, these professionals usually prefer to work with larger companies. You might do well to hire independent salespeople. Candle maker Melony Bell of Fort Meade, Florida, hired three such salespeople to work for her on a part-time basis to wholesale her candles to retail stores and sell retail to people they know.

Typically, salespeople work on commission, whether you hire them as an employee or an independent contractor. In either case, you need to clearly define the terms of your relationship at the very beginning to avoid any misunderstandings and possible litigation. The key points your sales rep agreement should cover include:

- *The rep's duties.* Clearly describe what you expect the rep to do to avoid any performance-related disputes. Do you expect him to make a minimum number of calls per day or per week? Are there certain types of customers you want targeted? Be specific.

- *Commission terms.* Define specifically how and when commissions are earned and calculated, when they are paid, whether the sales rep is expected to assist in collecting any money due, if delinquent accounts can affect commissions, and when commissions will end. Many states accept a doctrine of procuring cause, which means that if someone can demonstrate that he or she was responsible for bringing you a customer initially (the procuring cause of the business), then

▲

that person gets credit for all future business. This could mean that you would have to pay commissions to that person forever, unless your agreement clearly stipulates otherwise.

- *How the relationship can be terminated.* Specify how either party can end the rep relationship and what your mutual rights, obligations, and liabilities are. Include issues such as notice, severance, and return of company property.

- *Restrictive covenants.* On this topic, many business owners tend to think exclusively in terms of noncompete agreements, but other important restrictive covenants include confidentiality (which would prevent the disclosure of confidential company information) and no solicitation (which would prevent sales reps from calling on your customers if they go to work for someone else) agreements. It could be beneficial to make these points part of your contract.

- *Choice of laws provision.* Indicate which state laws will govern the agreement, and be sure the agreement meets the legal requirements of that state.

Selling on the Internet

Some crafters are doing very well selling on the Internet, some have invested substantially in creating Web sites and have sold very little, and even more have yet to venture out into the uncharted waters of cyberselling.

Ceramist Lynn Korff, who owns Korff's Ceramic Originals, sells exclusively over the Internet, and has been very happy with her results. When she first sold her shop

---

Going Once, Going Twice

The popularity of online auctions such as eBay as a sales avenue has grown tremendously in recent years. If you have a computer, modem, and either a digital camera or a scanner, you can quickly and easily put your crafts up for sale on an online auction site. Set your starting bid price (which is the lowest price you're willing to accept) and then let bidders drive up the final sale price as they compete for the privilege of buying your items.

Before you put an item up for auction, consider the shipping. Though typically the buyer pays the shipping costs, you still need to safely package the merchandise and arrange for shipment. Be sure you know what's involved, and be prepared to ship the item immediately after the auction closes and you have received payment.

For more about selling through online auctions, see Entrepreneur's Start-Up Guide #1824, *How to Start a Business on eBay.*

Where Can You Sell Your Crafts?

Crafts can be sold just about anywhere to anyone. The National Craft Association offers these ideas as just some of the ways to market or sell your creative products:

Places to sell retail
- ○ Arts and crafts fairs and shows
- ○ Private studios and workshops
- ○ Open house sales
- ○ Holiday boutiques
- ○ Seasonal boutiques
- ○ Home craft parties
- ○ Crafts consignment shops
- ○ Your own crafts co-op
- ○ Art galleries
- ○ Crafts malls and rent-a-space shops
- ○ Various local outlets including medical offices and hospitals, schools, retirement centers, small retail shops and service providers, special interest clubs, groups, or organizations
- ○ Mail order
- ○ Online

Places to sell wholesale
- ○ Trade shows
- ○ Selling through sales reps
- ○ Selling through gift marts
- ○ Selling direct to shops and galleries
- ○ Become a sales rep for your line and other compatible lines

Creating awareness of yourself and your products through promotional efforts
- ○ Enter contests
- ○ Write articles on your area of expertise for magazines
- ○ Write how-to arts or crafts booklets
- ○ Publish a newsletter for your market niche
- ○ Teach how-to techniques
- ○ Speak about your art or craft to groups
- ○ Become a local radio or TV personality as an expert in your field
- ○ Business-to-business and social networking
- ○ Cause, charity and/or community involvement
- ○ Get listed in all relative directories or guides
- ○ Join trade associations, guilds, or professional groups in your field
- ○ Do mailings to your customer list

▲

Bright Idea

If your product is bulky, or if you exhibit at shows where the customer base is tourists who must deal with packing and traveling home, offer to ship products from the show to their homes. The convenience will sway some on-the-fence shoppers and increase your sales.

and started doing custom ceramics from her home in Cabot, Pennsylvania, she thought she would have to sell items on consignment in local shops and do craft shows to generate the income she needed, but she was wrong. "I haven't had to do a single crafts show, and I haven't gone to a single store because the Web site took off," she says. "It's ideal because I don't have to leave my house if I don't want to." She credits the success of her Web site in large part to the fact that she hired a professional to promote the site and get it listed on search engines.

As more people gain access to the Internet and become more comfortable with computers as a shopping and decorating tool, online sales of crafts items should increase. See Chapter 9 in *Start-Up Basics* for more on developing a Web site.

Repeat Business

If you serve your customers properly, they'll come back to you when they need your products again. And it's much easier and more profitable to sell to an already satisfied customer than to a prospective customer who isn't sure about you. Repeat business is based not only on the admiration customers have for the quality or originality of your work, but also on your showing a genuine interest in them. You can help develop the customer loyalty that generates repeat business by being available to your customers, either in your studio or store, or at crafts shows in their area.

The factors that enable crafts businesses to maintain a high degree of customer loyalty are service, price, and selection. You need to have all three of these to be successful; if any or all are missing, you'll have to rely on sporadic business from one-time customers, and you won't survive that way for long.

Day-to-Day
Dollars and
Good Sense

For crafters, who by nature tend to be creative people more interested in their art than in administrative and financial details, managing the financial side of your operation may well be the most challenging part of being in business. However, one of the key indicators of the overall health of your business is its financial status, so it's important that you monitor your financial progress closely.

Even though you might start your crafts business on a very small scale, always keep in mind that it is a business, and as such, you should be keeping accurate records of your business dealings. This is not only legally required for tax, licensing, and insurance purposes, but it will help you follow customer orders and preferences, and give you the information you need to grow and be profitable.

Whether you work from home or a commercial site, and regardless of the type of bookkeeping system you use, your records must be permanent, accurate, and complete, and they must clearly establish income, deductions, credits, employee information (if applicable), and anything else specified by federal, state, and local regulations. If you have more than one business, the records for each must be complete and separate.

When you're getting started, it's very tempting to just stash your receipts in an envelope and promise yourself you'll remember various bits of income and expenditures—but that's setting up a foundation for failure. It's much easier to establish your record-keeping system properly from the start. You'll need to set it up only once, then maintain it as you go. Check out some of the computer accounting programs on the market; there are several that are affordable and easy to use. Or ask your accountant for help in setting up your system in a way that provides the detail you need and yet is easy enough for you to handle yourself.

Keeping good records helps generate the financial statements that tell you exactly where you stand and what you need to do next. The key financial statements you need to understand and use regularly are:

- *Income statement.* This is also called the profit and loss or P&L statement, which illustrates how much your company is making or losing over a designated

Ask Before You Need

Just about every growing business experiences economic rough spots and requires financing of some type sooner or later. Plan for the costs of growth and watch for signs of developing problems so you can figure out how to best deal with them before they turn into a major crisis.

Asking for money before you need it is especially important if you're going to be applying for a loan, whether it's from a private individual or a commercial loan source such as your bank. Most lenders are understandably reluctant to extend credit to a business in trouble. So plan your growth and pre-sell your banker on your financial needs. Such foresight demonstrates that you are an astute professional manager on top of every situation. Your chances of obtaining the funding you need will improve significantly.

period—monthly, quarterly, or annually—by subtracting expenses from revenue to arrive at a net result, which is either a profit or a loss. See the sample income statement on page 97.

- *Balance sheet.* A table showing your assets, liabilities, and capital at a specific point. A balance sheet is typically generated monthly, quarterly, or annually when the books are closed.

Smart Tip

Check the account status when you're taking an order from a customer on open credit. If the account is past due or the balance is unusually high, you may want to negotiate different terms before increasing the amount owed.

- *Cash flow statement.* This summarizes the operating, investing, and financing activities of your business as they relate to the inflow and outflow of cash. As with the profit and loss statement, a cash flow statement is prepared to reflect a specific accounting period, such as monthly, quarterly, or annually.

You should review these reports regularly, at least monthly, so you always know where you stand and can move quickly to correct minor difficulties before they become major financial problems. See Chapter 15 in *Start-Up Basics* for more on financial statements.

Billing

If you're extending credit to your customers—and it's likely you will if you sell on a wholesale basis—you need to establish and follow sound billing procedures.

Coordinate your billing system with your customers' payable procedures. Candidly ask what you can do to ensure prompt payment; that may include confirming the correct billing address and finding out what documentation may be required to help the customer determine the validity of the invoice. Keep in mind that many large companies pay certain types of invoices on certain days of the month. Find out if your customers do that, and schedule your invoices to arrive in time for the next payment cycle.

Most computer bookkeeping software programs include basic invoices. If you design your own invoices and statements, be sure they're clear and easy to understand. Detail each item, and indicate the amount due in bold with the words "Please pay" in front of the total. A confusing invoice may get set aside for clarification, and your payment will be delayed. See Chapters 8 and 14 in *Start-Up Basics* for more on computer invoicing programs.

Bright Idea

Use your invoices as a marketing tool. Print reminders of various items in your product line on them. Add a flier or brochure to the envelope—even though the invoice is going to an existing customer, you never know where your brochures may end up.

Setting Credit Policies

When you sell retail, you will rarely extend credit to individuals because they typically pay in full by cash, check, or credit card at the time of purchase. For most crafters, credit policies don't become an issue until they start selling at the wholesale level, because most businesses are not set up to pay at the time of delivery. You need to decide how much risk you are willing to take by setting limits on how much credit you will allow each account.

Keep this in mind as you develop your credit policies. By extending credit to a company, you are essentially providing an interest-free loan. You wouldn't expect someone to lend you money without getting information from you about where you live and work and your ability to repay. It just makes sense that you would want to get this information from someone you are lending money to.

Your accountant or attorney can help you develop a credit application, or you can use standard forms available in office supply stores. You want to at least get the company's full legal name, the names and titles of the owner(s), the actual address of the company (not just a post office box), phone and fax number, banking information, and references. Ideally, the references should be creditors similar to your business—just because a company pays its electric bill (something it must have to stay open) on time doesn't mean it'll pay a crafter on time. Always take the time to check the references. Write a letter or a place a phone call to their accounts receivable departments. And be sure the credit application is signed by a responsible individual with the company.

Reputable companies will not object to providing you with credit information, or even paying a deposit on large orders. If you don't feel comfortable asking for at least part of the money upfront, just think how uncomfortable you'll feel if you deliver an expensive order and don't get paid at all. You might feel awkward asking for deposits—until, that is, you get burned the first time, and then it won't be so difficult.

No Money, No Deal

For custom orders, be sure to get a deposit in advance. If any customers are reluctant to pay a deposit, it's a signal that they may not be willing to pay for the item when it's finished. Woodworker Jay Norman of DeLand, Florida, asks for a deposit that will at least cover the cost of materials so he's not out any cash if his customers change their minds after he's finished with their order. "Sometimes people ask me to make things that are not very common," he says, "and it's not like I can just take [those types of items] to a show and sell them."

Sample Income Statement

The income statement (or profit and loss statement) is a simple report on your company's cash-generating ability. You can prepare an income statement based on your company's actual performance, or, in the case of a new company, you can prepare a projected income statement as a forecasting and planning tool. This monthly income statement depicts the two hypothetical crafts businesses used for the equipment table in Chapter 8.

Item	Low	High
Gross sales	$1,084	$15,834
Cost of sales	115	5,250
Gross profit	$969	$10,584
Expenses		
Rent	$0	$300
Phone/utilities	15	125
Postage/delivery	4	35
Licenses/taxes	0	0
Owner/manager salary	700	3,500
Employees	0	2,500
Benefits/taxes	0	800
Advertising/promotion	15	225
Legal services	0	53
Accounting	25	58
Supplies	100	810
Maintenance	0	0
Transportation	14	110
Insurance	15	140
Subscriptions/dues	0	20
Depreciation	0	187
Miscellaneous	5	48
Total Expenses	**$893**	**$8,911**
Pretax Net Profit	**$76**	**$1,673**
Net Profit as a Percent of Gross Sales	**7%**	**10.6%**

Certainly extending credit involves some risk, but the advantages of judiciously granted credit far outweigh the potential losses. Extending credit promotes customer loyalty. People will call you instead of a competitor because they already have an account set up, and it's easy for them. Also, customers often spend money more easily when they don't have to pay cash. Finally, if you ever decide to sell your business, it will have a greater value because you can show steady accounts.

Your credit policy should include a clear collection strategy. Do not ignore overdue bills; the older a bill gets, the less likely it will ever be paid. Be prepared to take action on past due accounts as soon as they become past due.

Check and Re-Check

Just because a customer passed your first credit check with flying colors that doesn't mean you should never re-evaluate their credit status—in fact, you should do it on a regular basis.

Tell customers when you initially grant their credit application that you have a policy of reviewing accounts periodically so it's not a surprise when you do. Remember, things can change very quickly in the business world, especially in the retail environment, and a company that is on sound financial footing this year may be quite wobbly next year.

An annual re-evaluation of all customers on open account is a good idea—but if you start to see trouble in the interim, don't wait to take action. Another time to re-evaluate a customer's credit is when a credit line increase is requested.

Some key trouble signs are a slowdown in payments, increased merchandise returns, and difficulty getting answers to your payment inquiries. Even a sharp increase in ordering could signal trouble because companies concerned that they may lose their credit privileges may try to stock up while they can. Pay attention to what your customers are doing; a major change in their customer base or product line is something you may want to monitor.

Beware!
Your clients will frequently pay you in cash. You may be tempted to not report this revenue on your income tax return—but don't do it! Failing to report income is a crime and can cost you much more in the long run than you might save in the short term. Record and report all your income, no matter how it is received.

Take the same approach with a credit review as with a new credit application. Most of the time, you can use what you have on file to conduct the check, but if you're concerned for any reason, you may want to ask the customer for updated information.

Most customers will understand routine credit reviews and accept it as a sound business practice. A customer who objects may well have something to hide—and that's something you need to know.

Checking Out Checks

Most crafters accept personal checks without any problem, but it's a good idea to establish some procedures to protect yourself just in case the check is bad. Ask to see at least one piece of photo identification, and confirm that the address and telephone number printed on the check is correct. Make a photocopy of the check for your files before you deposit it.

Check with your bank for tips on avoiding fraudulent checks. There may be things your state needs for you to do when you accept the check that makes it possible for them to prosecute if the check bounces.

Accepting Cards

Many crafters say that the ability to accept credit cards increases their business substantially; others say it's too complicated and expensive for their small operations. For example, ceramist Lynn Korff, who runs Korff's Ceramic Originals out of Cabot, Pennsylvania, accepts credit cards because her sales are conducted online; candle maker Melony Bell of Fort Meade, Florida, used to accept credit cards, but stopped doing so because she didn't feel the additional sales were sufficient to justify the cost.

To accept credit cards, you need a merchant account, which is a special bank account that corresponds with a credit card processing company. The financial institution will put you through a process very similar to a credit application that determines your credit-worthiness and the legitimacy of your business. The process is similar for debit cards.

Credit and debit card service providers are widely available, so shop around to understand the service options, fees, and equipment costs. Expect to pay about $500 for a "swipe" machine that reads the magnetic strip on cards. You'll also pay a transaction charge, which might be a flat rate (perhaps 20 to 30 cents) per transaction or a percentage (typically 1.6 to 3.5 percent) of the sale. Expect to pay higher transactions fees for Internet and mail order sales, because the fraud risk the bank is accepting is higher than with face-to-face transactions.

If you do a lot of business at shows, consider a swipe machine with wireless communications capability, which allows you to get approval and complete the transaction from practically any location.

 Beware!

Don't be pressured into signing a long-term contract for debit and credit cards until you are sure what you need and want. Crafter Lynn Korff says she succumbed to such high-pressure sales tactics when she had her ceramics studio and ended up signing a four-year contract that was more service than she needed.

Be sure you get a written quote describing all the costs and charges associated with the merchant account so you aren't surprised when the first bill arrives. It's a good idea to deal with credit card services that specialize in dealing with crafters.

Your Own Creditors

Most business start-up advice focuses on dealing with your customers, but you're also going to become a customer for your suppliers. That means you'll have to pay for what you buy.

Find out in advance what your suppliers' credit policies are. Most will accept credit cards but won't put you on an open account until they've had a chance to run a check on you.

If you do open an account with a supplier, be sure you understand their terms and preserve your credit standing by paying on time. Typically, you'll have 30 days to pay, but many companies offer a discount if you pay early.

> **Dollar Stretcher**
>
> Ask suppliers if payment terms can be a part of your price negotiation. For example, can you get a discount for paying cash in advance?

A Taxing Business

A critical administrative element in retail sales is the collection and remittance of sales tax. In addition to state sales tax, you may also need to collect a local sales tax. Your state department of revenue will provide you with complete instructions for dealing with sales tax.

Failing to collect and remit sales taxes can lead to serious consequences, including fines and even criminal charges. Some small business owners think they are doing their customers a favor by not charging the appropriate sales tax, but in reality, you are breaking the law and taking a tremendous risk that could ultimately ruin your business.

If you operate by mail order or sell over the Internet, you may be required to collect and remit sales tax to the states where your customers reside. Check with your accountant for the latest rules on mail order sales tax requirements.

Remember: The sale isn't complete until the sales tax has been collected, reported, and paid to the proper government agency. Chapter 17 in *Start-up Basics* contains more information on sales tax.

Taxing Matters

Businesses are required to pay a wide range of taxes, and there are no exceptions for craft business owners. Keep good records so you can offset your local, state, and federal income taxes with the expenses of operating your company. If you have employees, you'll be responsible for payroll taxes. If you operate as a corporation, you'll have to pay payroll taxes for yourself; as a sole proprietor, you'll pay self-employment tax. Then there are property taxes, taxes on your equipment and inventory, fees and taxes to maintain your corporate status, your business license fee (which is really a tax), and other lesser-known taxes. Take the time to review all your tax liabilities with your accountant, and check out Chapter 17 in *Start-up Basics* for more information.

Tales from the Trenches

By now, you should know how to get started and have a good idea of what to do—and not do—in your own crafts business. But nothing teaches as well as the voice of experience. So we asked established craftspeople to tell us what has contributed to their success, and here's what they had to say.

Never Stop Learning

No matter how experienced you become, there will never be a time when you know it all. "Be prepared to learn as you go," says Jay Norman of Organize with Wood in DeLand, Florida. "Be as flexible in your thinking as possible."

Other crafters will be a great source of education for all aspects of your business, and most are willing to share what they know. Jay's wife, Dianne, offers one caveat: "Listen to other crafters, but if your item is different from theirs, put their advice into perspective."

Listen to Your Customers

Your customers will tell you want they want to buy. Sometimes they do it directly by asking for particular items. You should also listen to conversations among customers at craft shows and in stores. Jay and Dianne have used customer input to adjust certain designs, and sales have improved. "I kept hearing people say, 'If only this was in blue.' So at the next show, I had blue periwinkle flowered items, and sure enough, they sold," she says. "Listen to what people say, even if it's something you wouldn't put in your own home."

You can also "hear" your customers' preferences by what doesn't sell. Take a look at what you're bringing back from shows or what isn't moving in shops, and think about how you can change it. "If I have dolls left over at the end of the year, I redress them for next year," says Deb Farish, who owns Dolls by Deb in Manchester, Missouri. "Obviously, there was something missing, so I will make a new outfit to give them new life, and try to move them."

Note Fashion Trends

Browse through department stores when new seasonal lines are being introduced. Dianne recommends checking out the linen departments of upscale stores to see what the latest color trends are and using those colors in your home decor items. Also, read home decor and fashion magazines to get an idea of what's popular. "You need to do your research," she says.

Plan Shows Carefully

Find a healthy balance between doing as many shows as you can and giving yourself time to replenish your inventory.

Dianne says she and Jay spent the first summer they were in Florida at shows every weekend. "Then in the fall, we had no stock. December came, and we were totally wiped out. We couldn't fully supply the crafts store where we rent space." The following year, they planned better.

Deb and Judy Infinger, who runs Woods and Threads out of Altamonte Springs, Florida, limit themselves to fall shows and spend the rest of the year building their inventory. Do what works best for you.

Share Booths with Caution

You may try to save money by sharing your booth at a show with another crafter. That can work, but it can also be a disaster.

Deb travels and exhibits her dolls with her friend who makes baskets; the two product lines complement each other, and the partnership works well. But, cautions Judy, if your products don't mix well, your display will look strange and customers may be confused. Also, when sharing space, it's easy for the booth to get too crowded. "If you crowd your merchandise, nothing will get noticed," says Gladys Johnson of Dolls by Gladys in Bunn, North Carolina.

If you do decide to try a booth-sharing arrangement, be sure you work out all the details ahead of time: how merchandise is marked and displayed, who is responsible for what, and so on.

Avoid Reducing Prices

It may be tempting to reduce your prices at the end of a crafts show or on seasonal items to move merchandise, but crafters say that's not a good idea. "Never reduce your prices," says Deb. "I did it once or twice and was very sorry. Why all of a sudden is this doll not worth its price?" People will buy off-season merchandise even if it's not reduced, if they like and want it. Or you can store the items until the next show or season. Deb's experience proves that; she says, "I was selling witches after Halloween, and I didn't reduce the prices. If people like what you have, they're going to buy, regardless of the price. So don't sell yourself short."

If it becomes known that you routinely reduce prices at the end of a show, you'll have shoppers waiting until then—and your profits will be seriously reduced. And, adds Deb, by reducing prices, you're sending the message to customers that your products aren't worth the amount you originally had on them. "You should be proud of what you've done and not reduce the price."

▲

Learn to Say No

One of the hardest lessons for most crafters to learn is when to say no, but there are times when that's the best answer for yourself and your business. For example, it's flattering when a promoter asks you to exhibit at an event, but if the show isn't right for you, don't do it. You may be excited at the prospect of a large order, but if you can't increase your production while maintaining your quality and fill the order on time, turn the order down. You should also turn down work when you have reason to believe the customer can't pay for your products or services (or, you could ask for the money upfront). Finally, if you're not sure you're the right person for the project, if you're not comfortable that you have the skills and resources to do it right, then say no. In the long run, the respect you gain will be more valuable than any short-term profits might be.

Practice Packaging

Especially if you're going to be exhibiting in shows, you need to learn to pack efficiently. Because their wooden pieces are designed to be storage units of various types, Jay and Dianne pack the small items inside the larger ones. "We put the key racks inside the jewelry boxes, the jewelry boxes inside the chests, and the chests in the truck," Dianne says. You may be able to pack items inside your display or use certain items to pad others. When you're on the road, every inch of space is critical, so learn how to use it to its maximum benefit.

Change Your Products

If you want customers to come back and buy from you again, you need something different to sell. "We don't make the same thing over and over," says Jay. "Of course, if something works, we still make it, but at shows we always have something different, something new, even if it's small."

You might add a new product, or simply change something you're already doing. "When I look at one model doll that I made back when I first started, and I look at it today, I can see the evolution of the product based on what I've learned from making dolls over the years," says Deb.

Change Your Strategy

Your business strategy needs to evolve as the marketplace changes. Deb says when she first started doing shows, she would typically do 13 smaller shows during the fall season. "It was three weekends on, then one weekend off to recover and do laundry," she says. "The rents were very reasonable—usually $25, $35, or $50 for space." She recently decided to shift to doing fewer shows that are larger; the cost is higher, but so is the attendance, and those shows are typically promoted more heavily, which means higher sales.

Make It a Family Affair

Crafting is an excellent family business. Many crafters find their spouses have the administrative skills they lack. Youngsters appreciate the opportunity to express their creativity.

Deb says her children participate in her doll business. Her son makes one of her more simple designs, and her daughter developed a line of pillows for little dolls and butterflies that she sells. "They go to shows with me, they help me set up, they sew and paint, they make change and handle sales, they make suggestions. I'm raising two little entrepreneurs here," she says.

Accept Time Constraints

You have only 24 hours in a day, and you'll probably always have more ideas than you are able to implement. "There is never enough time to do all of the things you want to do," says Jay.

Walk Before You Run

Start small and grow your business as you gain knowledge and experience. "Start with the smaller, less expensive, nearby shows and learn how to make them work for you before you invest a lot in an expensive show that requires overnight travel," says candle maker Melony Bell of Fort Meade, Florida.

Do It for Yourself

Though serious crafters can make a comfortable income selling their work, it's highly unlikely you'll ever create Bill Gates–type wealth in this industry—which is why most crafters say the money is not what attracts them. "The most important thing is to love what you're doing and be proud of what you're doing," says Deb. "Do not let your success be measured solely in terms of dollars and cents. If you're doing it for the money, you're not doing it for the right reason."

Appendix
Crafts Business Resources

They say you can never be too rich or too thin. While these could be argued, we believe you can never have too many resources. Therefore, we present for your consideration a wealth of sources for you to check into, check out, and harness for your own personal information blitz.

These sources are tidbits, ideas to get you started on your research. They are by no means the only sources out there, and they should not be taken as the Ultimate Answer. We have done our research, but businesses do tend to move, change, fold, and expand. As we have repeatedly stressed, do your homework. Get out and start investigating.

As an additional tidbit to get you going, we strongly suggest the following: If you haven't yet joined the Internet Age, do it! Surfing the Net is like waltzing through a library, with a breathtaking array of resources literally at your fingertips.

Associations

American Ceramic Society, Box 6136, Westerville, OH 43086-6136, (614) 890-4700, www.acers.org

American Craft Association, 1927 Vanderhorn, Bartlett, TN 38134, (901) 507-1412, www.craftassociation.com

American Craft Council, 21 S. Eltings Corner Rd., Highland, NY 12528, (800) 836-3470, www.craftcouncil.org

▲

American Indian Arts and Crafts Association, 4010 Carlisle NE, Suite C, Albuquerque, NM 87107, (505) 265-9149, www.iaca.com

American Quilter's Society, Box 3290, Paducah, KY 42002, (270) 898-7903, www.aqsquilt.com

The Arts and Crafts Association of America, 4888 Cannon Woods Ct., Belmont, MI 49306, (616) 874-1721, www.artsandcraftsassoc.com

The Arts & Crafts Society, 1194 Bandera Dr., Ann Arbor, MI 48103, (734) 358-6882, www.arts-crafts.com

Association of Crafts & Creative Industries, P.O. Box 3388, Zanesville, OH 43702-3388, (740) 452-4541, www.creative-industries.com

Craft Emergency Relief Fund, provides immediate support to craftpeople suffering career-threatening emergencies such as fire, theft, natural disaster, and illness. Box 838, Montpelier, VT 05601, (802) 229-2306,www.craftemergency.org

Furniture Society, Box 18343, Asheville, NC 28814, (828) 255-1949, www.furniture society.org

Hand Papermaking Inc., Box 77027, Washington, DC 20013-7027, (301) 220-2393, www.handpapermaking.org

Handweavers Guild of America, 3327 Duluth Hwy., #201, Duluth, GA 30096-3301, (770) 495-7702,www.weavespindye.org

Hobby Industry Association, 319 E. 54th St., Elmwood Park, NJ 07407, (201) 794-1133, www.hobby.org

International Guild of Glass Artists Inc., 27829 365th Ave., Platte, SD 57369, www.igga.org

The Knifemakers' Guild, P.O. Box 265, Manti, UT 84642-0265, www.kmg.org

National Assembly of State Arts Agencies, 1029 Vermont Ave. NW, 2nd Fl., Washington, DC 20005, (202) 347-6352, TDD: (202) 347-5948, www.nasaa-arts.org

National Association of Artists' Organizations, c/o Space One Eleven, 2409 Second Ave., North, Birmingham, AL 35203-3809, (205) 251-2771, www.naao.net

National Association of Independent Artists, 2785 Stark Rd., Harris, MN 55032-3725, www.naia-artists.org

National Bead Society, Box 2293, Asheville, NC 28802, (888) 273-6298, www.national beadsociety.com

National Candle Association, 1156 15th St. NW, #900, Washington, DC 20005, (202) 393-2210, www.candles.org

National Council on Education for the Ceramic Arts, 77 Erie Village Square, #280, Erie, CO 80516, (866) 266-2322 or (303) 828-2811, www.nceca.net

National Craft Association, 1945 E. Ridge Rd., #5178, Rochester, NY 14622-2467, (800) 715-9594 or (716) 266-5472, www.craftassoc.com

National Institute of American Doll Artists, www.niada.org

The National Needlework Association, Box 3388, Zanesville, OH 43702-3388, (800) 889-8662, www.tnna.org

National Polymer Clay Guild, 1350 Beverly Rd, #115-345, McLean, VA 22101, (202) 895-5212, www.npcg.org

National Woodcarvers Association, P.O. Box 43218, Cincinnati, OH 45243, (513) 561-0627, www.chipchats.org

Society of American Silversmiths, P.O. Box 72839, Providence, RI 02907, (401) 461-6840, www.silversmithing.com

Society of North American Goldsmiths, 4513 Lincoln Ave., #213, Lisle, IL 60532-1290, (630) 852-6385, www.snagmetalsmith.org

Stencil Artisans League Inc., P.O. Box 3109, Los Lunas, NM 87031, (505) 865-9119, e-mail: salihelp@aol.com, www.sali.org

Woodworking Association of North America, P.O. Box 478, Depot Rd., Tamworth, NH 03886, (603) 323-7500, http://wana.freeyellow.com

Consultants and Other Experts

Robert S. Bernstein, Esq, Bernstein Bernstein Krawec & Wymard, 1133 Penn Ave., Pittsburgh, PA 15222, (412) 456-8100, e-mail: bob@bernsteinlaw.com

Vicki L. Helmick, CPA, 1312 Sterling Oaks Dr., Casselberry, FL 32792, (407) 695-3400, www.accountant-city.com/viki-helmick-cpa

Credit Card and Other Payment Processing Services

American Express Merchant Services, (888) 829-7302, www.americanexpress.com

Arts and Crafts Business Solutions, Guy McDonald, (800) 873-1192

Discover Card Merchant Services, (800) 347-6673

MasterCard, (914) 249-4843, www.mastercard.com

PayPal, www.paypal.com

VeriSign Payment Services, (888) 847-2747, www.verisign.com

Visa, www.visa.com

▲

Equipment and Supplies

All About Dolls, doll making supplies for porcelain, vinyl, and soft body dolls, 72 Lakeside Blvd., Hopatcong, NJ 07843,(973) 770-3228, www.allaboutdolls.com

All Seasons Trading Co., jewelry supplies, 888 Brannan, #1160, San Francisco, CA 94103, (415) 864-3308, www.allseason.com

American Crafters, lace and ribbon distributor, 29722 Merjanian Rd., Menifee Valley, CA 92584, (800) 326-5223 or (909) 679-0526, www.americancraftersoutlet.com

B*Country, desktop tools and publishing services, 509 Teton Dr., Jerome, ID 83338, (877) 281-5138, www.bcountry.net

Dharma Trading Co., textile crafts supplies, P.O. Box 150916, San Rafael, CA 94915, (800) 542-5227 or (415) 456-7657, www.dharmatrading.com

Fetpak Inc., displays, bags, boxes, packaging, and shipping supplies, 70 Austin Blvd., Commack, NY 11725, (800) 883-3872, www.fetpak.com

J.S. Ritter Jewelers Supply, 118 Preble St., Portland, ME 04101, (800) 962-1468, www.jsritter.com

Nimrod Hall Copper Co., copper foil and tooling copper, HCR 4 Box 31, Millboro, VA 24460, (703) 447-6509, www.nimrodhall.com

Smokey Mountain Woodcarvers Supply, P.O. Box 82, Townsend, TN 37882, (865) 448-2259, www.woodcarvers.com

Stained Glass Warehouse, stained glass supplies and tools, P.O. Box 609, Arden, NC 28704-0609, (828) 650-0992, www.stainedglasswarehouse.com

Wood-n-Crafts Inc., craft and woodworking products, P.O. Box 140, Lakeview, MI 48850, (989) 352-8075, www.wood-n-crafts.com

Government Agencies and Related Resources

Library of Congress, Copyright Office, 101 Independence Ave. SE, Washington, DC 20559-6000, (202) 707-3000, www.loc.gov/copyright

U.S. Patent and Trademark Office, Washington, DC 20231, (800) 786-9199 or (703) 308-4357, www.uspto.gov

Online Services and Resources

Crafts Fair OnLine, www.craftsfaironline.com, a Web site with links to a wide range of crafts sites for supplies, materials, software, publications, shows, instructions, and more, www.craftsfaironline.com

Craft Smarts, a Web site with information about the business of crafts, www.crafts-marts.com

StarvingArtistsLaw.com, a central location for artists and writers looking for self-help legal information and links to state Volunteer Lawyers for the Arts organizations, www.starvingartistslaw.com

Publications

Arts & Crafts Show Business, monthly listing of shows in FL, GA, NC, and SC, Box 26624, Jacksonville, FL 32226, (904) 757-3913, www.artscraftsshowbusiness.com

Art & Craft Show Yellow Pages, quarterly guide to shows in CT, MA, NJ, NY, PA, and VT, Box 484-W, Rhinebeck, NY 12572, (845) 876-2995, www.choices.cc

Clay Times Magazine, Box 365, 15481 Second St., Waterford, VA 20197, (540) 882-3576, www.claytimes.com

Craftmaster News, monthly listing of West Coast shows, Box 39429, Downey, CA 90239, (562) 869-5882, www.craftmasternews.com

Crafts Fair Guide, quarterly listing of West Coast shows, Box 688, Corte Madera, CA 94976, (800) 871-2341 or (415) 924-3259, www.craftfairguide.com

Crafts Report, print and online magazine with show listings, 300 Water St., Box 1992, Wilmington, DE 19899, (800) 777-7098 or (302) 656-2209, www.craftsreport.com

Interweave Press, publications on beading, knitting, needlework, spinning, weaving, Box 2626, San Anselmo, CA 94979, (800) 272-2193, www.interweave.com

Ronay Guides, three annual publications listing shows, fairs and festivals in GA, SC, NC, and VA, 2090 Shadow Lake Dr., Buckhead, GA 30625, (706) 342-8225, www.events2000.com

SAC Newsmonthly, monthly listing of shows across the country, Box 159, Bogalusa, LA 70429-0159, (800) 825-3722, www.sacnewsmonthly.com

Show West, monthly listing of shows in AZ, CA, CO, MN, NV, and UT, Box 6278, Phoenix, AZ 85005, (623) 873-3350, www.showwestmag.com

Specialty Retail Report, magazine for cart and kiosk retailers, 293 Washington St., Norwell, MA 02061, (800) 936-6297, www.specialtyretail.com

Sunshine Artist, monthly listing of shows, 3210 Dade Ave., Orlando, FL 32804, (407) 228-9772, www.sunshineartist.com

Woodworker's Journal, Box 56585, Boulder, CO 80322-6585, (800)765-4119, www.woodworkersjournal.com

Successful Crafts Business Owners

Anita A. Fetter, 7490 Madden Road, Waynesfield, OH 45896, (419) 648-3461

Dolls by Deb, Deborah Farish, 905 Chestnut Ridge, Manchester, MO 63021, e-mail: dollsbydeb@yahoo.com

Dolls by Gladys, Gladys Johnson, 16 Alford Mill Road, Bunn, NC, 27508, (919) 496-0112

Korff's Ceramic Originals, Lynn Korff, 1229 Cornplanter Rd., Cabot, PA 16023, (877) 446-0847, www.korfforiginals.com

Organize with Wood, Jay and Dianne Norman, 528 N. High St., DeLand, FL 32720, (904) 740-9836

Wood and Threads, Judy Infinger, 611 Little Wekiva Rd., Altamonte Springs, FL 32716, (407) 682-5490

Glossary

Acrylic paint: color pigment in a nontoxic, water-based formula that cleans up with soap and water

Aida cloth: the most popular cross-stitch fabric, this cloth is made of threads woven in groups and separated by tiny holes which creates a pattern of squares across the fabric surface that a beginning cross-stitcher can easily follow

Airbrush: an atomizer that uses compressed air to spray liquid

Appliqué: in most crafts, this is the process of applying an item to another finished item; it is also used to describe the item to be applied

Archival-quality paper: an acid-free, nonyellowing paper that resists early deterioration

Backing: fabric used for the bottom layer of a quilt

Base candle: a molded or hand-formed candle on which a more elaborate candle is built

Base coat: the first application of paint on a surface, often in preparation for more detailed decorative painting to follow

Basting: long, loose stitches that can be easily removed

Batik: a method of dyeing fabric in which some areas are covered with wax or pastes made of glues or starches that prevent dyes from penetrating in those areas

Batting: used primarily for lining quilts or stuffing pillows and dolls, this material comes in sheets of raw cotton, wool, or polyester

Beeswax: a natural wax derived from honey bee hives; used in candle-making and to strengthen and smooth beading thread in jewelry making

Bias: the diagonal of a piece of fabric

Block candle: any candle made with a mold

Blocking: the process of straightening and squaring a fabric or canvas piece, usually by stretching and securing the edges to a wooden frame when the piece is damp then letting it dry

Brush basin or tub: a container with two or three sections for cleaning paint brushes, which also has slots for holding brushes both in and out of liquid

Cane: a long rod of glass or clay, patterned or plain, used to make beads

Consignment: a method of selling goods in which the owner places the goods in the possession of a third party (typically a retailer) who displays and sells the merchandise, then retains a percentage of the sales price for their effort

Container: in candle-making, anything used to pour a candle in that is to be used as an integral part of the candle, as opposed to a mold from which the candle is removed before use

Cording: consisting of strands of embroidery floss or yarn that's been woven or twisted together, cording is ideal for adding a finished border to a needlecrafts project

Core: the central portion of a candle

Crosscutting/miter cutting: sawing across the wood grain to reduce a board's length; a crosscut at an angle other than 90 degrees to the board's edge is a miter cut

Danish taper: a long, thin, curved candle with lots of additives in the wax

Decoupage: an art form that involves cutting out paper images, gluing them to a surface, then applying a coat of finish to create the illusion of hand-painting or inlay

Dip tank: any large container, filled with either hot wax or cold water, into which a candle is dipped

Embossing: raising an image above the surface of an item

Embroidery hoops: two plastic or wooden rings that fit tightly inside each other

Essential oil (EO): natural extracts of plant matter

Even-weave fabric: fabric that has the same distance between the warp and weft threads

Faux: false, fake, imitation

Ferrule: the metal ring around a paintbrush that strengthens the handle at the end holding the bristles

Findings: all types of fasteners and construction components used in jewelry-making

Floral foam: porous green foam typically used to hold flowers in place for arrangements

Floss: the six-ply cotton thread most often used for cross-stitch

Fragrance oil (FO): a synthetic or synthetic/natural blend of oil

Fusible webbing: strong, narrow, closely woven tape that is bonded to fabric with heat

Gilt: gold plating

Glow-through candle: any candle with an unmelted outer shell through which light glows

Graphite paper (black or white): special artist's transfer paper used for transferring a traced pattern onto a wood piece

Hanging sleeve: a tube or sleeve sewn to the back top of a quilt to allow it to be hung on a wall or at a quilt show; shows request these to be 3 to 4 inches wide

Hot-glue gun: a tool that melts glue sticks and releases an easy-to-control line of glue

Kiln: a furnace or oven built of heat-resistant materials for firing pottery or sculpture

Lapidary: cutting, shaping, polishing, and creating jewelry from precious and semi-precious stones

Metallic ribbon: an iridescent, reflective ribbon available in many colors and widths

Mold: any form that can be used to shape fluid or plastic substances

Natural sea sponge: a type of sponge that can create a dappled, textured look when used to apply paint

Needle-punched batting: a manufacturing process used to make quilt batting of cotton or wool where thousands of barbed needles are punched through the carded fibers to lock them into position to prevent shifting of the batting in the finished quilt

Needlework frame: a frame consisting of roller bars to which fabric can be attached then rolled in opposite directions to tighten

Overcast stitching: a simple whip stitch that prevents fabric from raveling while it is being worked on

▲

Palette knives: knives made from stainless steel or flexible plastic designed for mixing paint on a palette

PFD fabric: stands for "prepared for dyeing"; a fabric with no surface finish and no treatment so the dyes can penetrate

Pin stem: the sharp pin part on the back of a brooch or pin

Rickrack: a flat, woven braid that creates a zigzag border when it's stitched onto fabric

Rotary cutter and mat: a fabric-cutting tool with a circular blade that cuts through several layers of fabric at once

Seam allowance: the distance between the outside (cut) edge of a piece of fabric and the stitching line

Stearic acid: a mild, noncorrosive acid made from animal fats and used to brighten candle colors, strengthen wax, and improve mold release

Stencil overlays: multiple-stencil designs used to apply a motif in sequential layers

Tack cloth: a specially treated cloth that removes sanding residue and dust particles from wood surfaces

Tapestry needles: needles with a blunt end and large eye that can hold multiple plies of floss or thick yarn

Tea-dying: a dying technique involving soaking fabric in a gallon of warm tea for about 15 minutes then line drying; when the fabric is dried and ironed, it has a soft, aged appearance

Technical pens: used for pen-and-ink projects, these pens draw crisp, permanent-inked lines that won't bleed onto acrylic paint

Topiary: the cutting or training of trees, bushes, shrubs, or artificial flowers into decorative shapes for landscaping or crafts projects

Transfer printing: using a special paper with a coating to transfer a design printed by an inkjet printer or color copier to a fabric

Vitreous: having the nature of glass

Warp: the threads that are put on a loom under tension and are raised and lowered to allow the weft to pass through

Wash: acrylic paint mixed with water or a medium (1:5 ratio) that provides a transparent look

Weft: the woven threads in a fabric that run across the width of the fabric during weaving and intersect with the warp threads

Index

Start-Up Guides
Books
Software

To order our catalog call 800-421-2300.
Or visit us online at smallbizbooks.com